T0168351

Walking Shadows

The newly bearded Orson Welles arrives in Hollywood, July 21, 1939, to be greeted at the airport by a crowd of reporters.

Walking Shadows

Orson Welles, William Randolph Hearst, and *Citizen Kane*

John Evangelist Walsh

THE UNIVERSITY OF WISCONSIN PRESS

POPULAR PRESS

The University of Wisconsin Press
1930 Monroe Street
Madison, Wisconsin 53711

www.wisc.edu/wisconsinpress/

3 Henrietta Street
London WC2E 8LU, England

1   3   5   4   2

Printed in the United States of America

Library of Congress Cataloging-in-Publication Data
Walsh, John Evangelist, 1927–
Walking shadows : Orson Welles, William Randolph Hearst,
and *Citizen Kane* / John Evangelist Walsh.
p.   cm.
"A Ray and Pat Browne book."
Includes bibliographical references and index.
ISBN 0-299-20500-2 (cloth: alk. paper)
1. Citizen Kane (Motion picture)   I. Title.
PN1997.C51173W35   2004
791.43′72—dc22   2004005370

Also by John Evangelist Walsh

The Execution of Major Andre

Moonlight: Abraham Lincoln and the Almanac Trial

Darkling I Listen: The Last Days and Death of John Keats

Midnight Dreary: The Mysterious Death of Edgar Allan Poe

Unraveling Piltdown: The Science Fraud of the Century and Its Solution

The Shadows Rise: Abraham Lincoln and the Ann Rutledge Legend

This Brief Tragedy: Unraveling the Todd-Dickinson Affair

Into My Own: The English Years of Robert Frost

The Bones of St. Peter: The First Full Account of the Search for the Apostle's Body

Night on Fire: The First Complete Account of John Paul Jones' Greatest Battle

Plumes in the Dust: The Love Affair of Edgar Allan Poe and Fanny Osgood

One Day at Kitty Hawk: The Untold Story of the Wright Brothers and the Airplane

The Hidden Life of Emily Dickinson

The Shroud

Strange Harp, Strange Symphony: The Life of Francis Thompson

Poe the Detective: The Curious Circumstances Behind *The Mystery of Marie Roget*

Fiction

The Man Who Buried Jesus

Out, out, brief candle!
Life's but a walking shadow, a poor player,
That struts and frets his hour upon the stage,
And then is heard no more.

—*Macbeth*

Dedicated
with love to the two
who can remember with me
the teeming life on
New York's
Amsterdam Avenue
where it all began,
my sister,
PATRICIA,
and my brother,
BILL,
and to the memory
of my brother,
TOM

Contents

Contents

Acknowledgements

My first thanks, as always, go to all those who handled this subject before me—reporters, writers, editors, biographers, commentators, and critics of all stripes, some sixty years' worth of them. Their good work, now on record for all to see and use, made my own task infinitely easier. My debt to them may be read in the bibliography and the notes.

More particularly I thank:

My son Timothy A. Walsh, whose incisive reading of the manuscript unerringly picked out its soft spots; my son John C. Walsh for various forms of timely aid; Tammy Ferdula, *The Day* (Conn.); Philip Pavel, the Marmont Hotel, Los Angeles; the Kenosha (Wisc.) Public Library; Don Jensen and Tom Gunderson, *Kenosha News;* the Theater Collection, the Wisconsin Historical Society, Madison; Memorial Library, University of Wisconsin–Madison; Tony Bliss, Bancroft Library, University of California, Berkeley; Lilly Library, Indiana University (Welles Collection). A special thanks to the accommodating and cheerfully efficient staff of the Monroe (Wisc.) Public Library, Lisa Cihlar, Director, and librarians Linda Bourquin, Ann Mueller, Maggie Guralski, Nancy Myers, Donna Oxenreider, and Rita Grinnell.

To my wife Dorothy I am indebted for various patient sufferances.

Prologue
His Hour

Just where on the list of great movies the much-praised *Citizen Kane* deserves to be placed, whether at the very top or lower down or not at all, isn't a question that particularly interests me. No doubt that's because I'm not a professional critic or student of film, only a simple moviegoer who happens to be a writer of history.

There are those—movie people mostly, intimately concerned with the art of filmmaking—who in polls usually give *Kane* the top spot, hailing it as filmdom's finest achievement. But that's only one view of the question. Among the public in general—ticket buyers happily unaware of technicalities such as camera angles and depth of focus—it fares less well. In any case I am content to agree that *Kane,* with all its obvious faults, certainly belongs among the best movies ever made, in its own way singularly powerful and evocative, not forgetting influential.

What does considerably interest me are the circumstances that gave rise to the picture, and which attended its fortunes thereafter. Especially intriguing, to me at any rate, is the truly startling fact that it was the product of a newcomer to Hollywood, a neophyte twenty-four-year-old who, in his first effort at movie-making, did something no one could have predicted. Coolly and deliberately, in the process of making his hugely innovative film, without any apparent need or reason, he chose to mount an attack on one of the day's most formidable public figures, targeting his private not primarily his public character.

As is well known, the rabid opposition of that figure, the fabulously wealthy newspaper tycoon William Randolph Hearst, came perilously close to destroying the picture, after it was made but before it was released. The resulting public battle, inevitably, brought it forcibly to public attention, sparking the most elaborate prerelease publicity ever enjoyed by a movie. Yet, despite such a dramatic start, despite the chorus of critical praise it met on finally reaching the theaters, it sorely disappointed its financial backers. It was a box office flop.

But even those arresting circumstances don't fully express the reason for my interest in the matter. Besides its being a unique slice of theatrical history, I see *Kane* as a whale of a story, and not just because it invokes the unfailing fascination of Hollywood. Here in almost classic form is a tale of youthful ambition, riding a marvelous array of talents, finding itself suddenly, wonderfully triumphant—only to be sorely humbled and eventually crushed by the very array of talents that had gained the victory in the first place.

Strangely like Hamlet, one of his heroes, the variously gifted Orson Welles, *Kane*'s originator, director, producer, and star, as well as its cowriter, while ready to dare all, in the end found that regarding himself and his future he simply could not make up his mind. Again like Hamlet, that painful indecision was to cost him his life, his working life as creator, performer, and full-blown theatrical force.

A striking combination of personal qualities and creative flare, Welles was that rare show business creature, a true *phenomenon*. Possessor of high intelligence, wide knowledge, and remarkably varied artistic and theatrical abilities, he was also a fine natural performer on the stage and an original force in radio. Impressive physically in the tall, dark, and handsome mold, he had a deep, commanding voice richly timbred, a glib tongue, and a bravura temperament, all wrapped in an unfailing self-confidence. Add the fact of his youth (a child prodigy, he garnered his first newspaper publicity at age ten), and the picture is complete of a man who *should* have earned a lofty and unchallenged place as a major figure in the history of world cinema and theater. But he didn't.

After *Kane,* for Welles there stretched the sad and puzzling spectacle of forty-four years of artistic vagabondage. Behind him when he died in 1985 lay a trail of

broken commitments and unfinished projects, sprinkled with a few minor successes. Only occasionally
were those latter years lit by a brief flare-up of the old
brilliance.

None of this is new, of course. Describing and explaining the surprising failure of Orson Welles after
Kane has been the aim of many pens during the inter-
vening decades. *Kane*'s link with Hearst and the fight
between the two have also been much described and
dissected. Yet all those previous treatments of the
Welles-Hearst-*Kane* story leave a good deal out, doing
little more than picking up and passing along a certain
limited amount of bare fact. The role of Welles in the
story predominates, with the formidable Hearst becoming hardly more than a menacing shadow in the
background, just one more showbiz villain. Small effort is made to add to the story or to ground it on solid
documentation, making precise what has been approx-
imate and annoyingly fuzzy.

The full story of this pivotal episode in Hollywood
history, in other words, has yet to be told.

Most particularly, the part played by the vengeful
William Randolph Hearst and his many willing abet-
tors in their bitter, months-long anti-*Kane* campaign
stands in need of more searching study. His probable
manipulation of the 1942 Academy Awards, for instance, and his link to the sad downfall of *Kane*'s female
lead, Dorothy Commingore, cry out for investigation.
The formidable Hearst, who was careful to operate

from cover throughout the nasty fight, has long managed to dodge his full share of guilt and responsibility. More than that, by lurking in the background as he did he worked a dire disservice to himself, inviting permanent damage to his reputation. After all, *Citizen Kane* did massively invade his personal life, his well-guarded privacy, exposing him to public contempt and ridicule. The admitted fact that this rough treatment only repeated what Hearst himself in his fifty-year journalistic rampage had done to many others isn't really a sufficient answer, at least not in this case.

In the Hollywood code of the time it was well understood and agreed that the private lives of studio executives, and others behind the cameras, were just that, private, and as such exempt from prying or exposure on any basis. Hearst, it must be remembered, in addition to all his other interests and pursuits, was every bit as much a movie mogul as were his friends who ran MGM, Warner's, Fox, and Paramount. Legitimately, he could expect the same protection as was accorded them. Especially could he assume immunity from anyone who made his living in the movie industry itself!

Between my handling of the subject and prior offerings there is a further difference of approach, of method, I should perhaps explain. That is my occasional use of straight narrative in place of standard historical exposition, in which I give the *results* of my studies without stopping in the main text to argue the underlying proofs. Where sufficient documentary evidence is available, and where the documents are rich in life-giving detail, either stated or implied, I prefer the immediacy of narrative to the more distant expository method of the traditional historian. I prefer to *show* what happened, of course meaning show it as *I* see it on the evidence.

That must not, however, be taken as implying any least shade or taint of fiction in what follows. In these pages literally everything said or suggested rests on authentic sources, whether it is the lift of an eyebrow, the location of a house, the hour of the day, or who did or said what and where. But I don't, as I say, burden the main text with argument. Instead, in the extensive notes section will be found all my sources fully cited and identified, along with elaboration of those points having special interest or importance. Occasionally I tell parts of the story through dialogue reconstructed from actual, known thoughts. Here too the notes give my authority as well as background.

It is the famous Rosebud symbolism pervading *Citizen Kane* and bringing it to its memorable conclusion in those final seconds, that perhaps tells most about both Hearst and Welles. Or say that best opens the door to a truer appreciation of each in their mutual struggle.

The usual interpretation of the Rosebud sled symbolism sees it as signaling the underlying cause of Kane's ruthless, self-gratifying character. The traumatic childhood experience in which he was suddenly torn from his parents' home, losing their love and never afterwards knowing true warmth or affection, is deftly wrapped up in the sled's Rosebud trademark. That is what the movie itself seems to imply, in fact comes close to stating outright. But I think the meaning is a bit more tangled than that, sunk a little deeper in the individual personality.

"Rosebud," it seems to me, stands not for any *outward* circumstance. It stands for Kane's *own* culpability, his own willful corruption of the purity of heart he possessed as an innocent boy. The mournfully whispered "Rosebud" falling from the lips of the dying Kane calls up his carefree youth when happiness was an ordinary sled in the snow, with unlimited hours to revel in the spacious white (unsullied) world around him. Seen by Kane more vividly because of the little snow-filled glass globe in his hand, that flash of memory awakens in the moribund tycoon a last, sad realization of what he *might* have made of himself, and didn't. Of course that is often the way of old men looking back who have gained the whole world at the cost of their souls.

There it was that the essential truth about Hearst himself is caught and cruelly mirrored in the movie, and one moment in particular I think reflects it—when Kane after smashing up Susan's bedroom pauses to gaze blankly at the little glass globe in his hand. It was that damning implication more than any other, I believe, which brought the full force of Hearst's wrath down on the interloper Welles and his great but too-disturbing picture, especially so if the very personal meaning of Rosebud for Hearst really was what contemporary report claims it to have been, a possibility treated in chapter 4.

In another, quite curious way—but without implying any of the malevolence that marred Hearst—that self-same observation may be applied to Welles, both while he was making *Kane* and afterward. Years later he was to confess that, as a child prodigy, "the word *genius* was whispered into my ear" so often by so many people that "it never occurred to me until middle age that I wasn't."

He laughed when he said it, as the interviewer reports. But it wasn't at all meant as a joke. It was nothing more or less than the plain, honest if painful truth. Much about the daring young man, who was often in those days dubbed "the boy wonder," not always as a compliment, is explained by it. From a very early age, as a result of his truly astonishing precocity, Welles learned a fatal lesson, that he could nearly always get away with pleasing himself alone. It was an attitude he never lost, but which grew with the years, becoming both a blessing and a curse. From it came all of his remarkable early triumphs on the stage and in radio and pictures, while making quite inevitable his eventual failure.

Curiously, though the word Rosebud has no known link to Welles' personal life, by his own admission his childhood did conceal one poignant memory of that sort. Like Hearst's Rosebud, it served as a bittersweet reminder of youthful dreams gone wrong. Unlike Hearst's, it carried no hint that for success he'd traded his soul—which was never possessed by anyone but himself—only a little of his common humanity. Rather than reveal it here, we'll save it for its proper place, where all true Rosebuds are found out, the end of the story.

Walking Shadows

I

Sneak Preview

From inside the thick bars of the high, wrought-iron gate the uniformed guard peered at the familiar face. "Good evening, Miss Hopper," he said, pulling open the smaller door at the side. Flashing a smile of thanks, the trim, middle-aged woman walked through the door, continued along the broad main street of the spacious RKO lot, then entered a building. At the projection room she was greeted by another guard, who swung the door wide for her. "They're waiting for you, Miss Hopper," he said.

Covering one end of the long, narrow room was a screen, and facing it were several rows of plush chairs. In the wall behind the chairs rose the projection booth. As Miss Hopper entered she saw that in the seats were only five others, all men, one of whom rose to greet her. He towered almost a foot over the tall Miss Hopper.

"Hedda, you made it. I'm glad!" said Orson Welles, who then turned and introduced the others: Herb Drake, his publicity man, Dick Pollard of *Life* magazine, Jim Crow of *Look,* and Doug Churchill of the *New York Times.*

All four said hello as Miss Hopper turned back toward Welles, looking surprised. "Is that all?" she asked. "I thought this was supposed to be a full press screening. Where is everybody? Where's Louella? Don't tell me you left her out! Wait till she hears!"

"For tonight, yes, that's all," replied Welles. *Life* and *Look* needed more lead time than the others to get something in their mid-February issues, when the picture was to be released. The *Times* was there by courtesy and would hold the story. More preliminary screenings were planned, he added, for the rest of the press, for distributors, exhibitors, and so on. "Louella we'll invite to the next one. She'll understand."

"I doubt it! In this morning's *Reporter* there was an item about your showing the picture tonight."

"I saw it. Didn't come from us."

"Release is in mid-February?"

"The fourteenth, we hope. That gives us only some six weeks to finish. Not much time and we still have *lots* to do! As I've already told these men, you won't hear any music with the film tonight. Scoring's not ready. Some other things we haven't decided yet. So *please* remember that we're giving you a preliminary look, the very *first* look outside the studio."

4

Miss Hopper took a seat as Welles gestured up to the projectionist. "Let's go," he directed, then to his guests he said, "Thanks for coming. Now I'll leave you alone."

As the lights in the room went down, Welles took his coat and hat and walked out.

On the screen appeared RKO's familiar noisy trademark, a tall radio tower atop a globe of the world giving off a staccato rush of signals. Then abruptly the tower disappeared and on the still-darkened screen there were large white letters spelling "A MERCURY PRODUCTION," and on a separate line "BY ORSON WELLES." Then appeared the title, two short words in plain, square lettering that filled the entire screen from top to bottom: "CITIZEN KANE."

Next appeared a small rectangular sign affixed to a gate, the background lightening but still murky: NO TRESPASSING. Up the tall gate travels the camera to a large K in a circle adorning the very top. Past the gate, high in the distance is seen an enormous mansion set on a hill, all dark except for one lighted window. Slowly, steadily toward that light moves the camera. . . .

For the next two hours the five viewers sat spellbound as a succession of strikingly original scenes and images mercilessly laid bare the private life of the fabulously wealthy newspaper tycoon Charles Foster Kane. At its finish, in the last moments the camera picks up a boy's sled as it is thrown into the flames of a furnace by a workman, and a swift close-up discloses on it the

5

printed brand-name Rosebud. In the finished picture, that revealing instant is anticipated by a rising crescendo of music, climaxed by a triumphal clash as the name is at last clearly shown. At the preview in the RKO studios on January 3, 1941, there was no music, so the moment of revelation had something less than its full impact.

In the view of three of those watching, the lack of music didn't matter. Each went home to write a glowing review of what he'd seen. Dick Pollard's comments, eventually printed in *Life,* give a good sampling of what was felt by all three:

> Few movies have ever come from Hollywood with such powerful narrative, such original technique, such exciting photography. Director Welles and cameraman Gregg Toland do brilliantly with a camera everything Hollywood has always said you couldn't do. They shoot into bright lights, they shoot into the dark and against low ceilings, till every scene comes with the impact of something never seen before. Even the sound track is new. And for narrative Welles has tapped a segment of life fearfully skirted by the U.S. cinema: the swift and brutal biography of a power-mad newspaper tycoon, a man of twisted greatness who buys or bullies his way into everything but friends' love or his nation's respect. . . . Skeptics about Mr. Welles may now relax. His eighteen months in Hollywood have not been wasted.

Left vastly unimpressed by what she saw that night was Miss Hedda Hopper, one of Hollywood's two leading gossip columnists. As a technical achievement, she felt, the picture was nothing to crow about: the photography was "old-fashioned," the writing and the dialogue "very corny," the whole thing a trial to sit through as entertainment. But that reaction was conditioned by the fact that the picture also left her surprised, not a little shocked, and openly angry, "appalled," was her word for it.

At every turn of events in the film, with every veiled reference and broad innuendo, she recognized her friend William Randolph Hearst (who had "always been unfailingly kind" to her, as she put it, who had several times expressed his admiration of her work, and often invited her to his sumptuous home as a pampered guest). Welles too she had known for some years, though not intimately. Occasionally she'd run into him back in New York during her brief try at the stage, once filling a small part in a play in which he'd starred. That was before she began the movie-land column that eventually made her a power in the business.

Disturbed, uncertain what she should do about the situation, if anything, she had, as she later recalled, much trouble getting to sleep that night. Hearst had his faults, God knows, she kept thinking, but to stand by and see him pilloried like this? To see his name and his character, *private* character, trashed? To see his mind and emotions portrayed as horribly warped, degenerate almost? He had his faults but he wasn't *all* bad. . . .

7

William Randolph Hearst at about the time he tried to prevent *Citizen Kane* from reaching the public, offering to buy it for a million dollars and then doing his best to kill it.

Early next morning her phone rang, and when she heard the deep-voiced Orson Welles on the other end asking what she thought of his movie she told him. The movie was a complete disgrace, "an impudent, murderous trick to perpetrate on a man who'd been a newspaper giant for twice as long as a certain boy genius had been alive!"

Why on earth did he want to blacken the Hearst name, to expose a man's personal, private life to such a load of mockery and scorn? But Welles had better be warned. Soon enough if he went ahead with the picture he'd find he was making a very bad mistake in taking on a man like Hearst.

"Hearst? Hearst? Who said anything about Mr. Hearst? What makes you think my movie has anything to do with your good friend the Lord of San Simeon?"

"Never mind, Orson, you won't get away with it," she answered. Hearst would certainly bring suit, she added, might even take steps to prevent the movie's release. Junking it would cause a huge financial loss, which might easily kill Welles' Hollywood career before it got started. Everybody knew that RKO wasn't in the best of shape financially. Everybody knew that Welles had been brought out from New York and given that fabulous contract precisely in order to help rescue the faltering studio.

"Orson, I'm sorry for you. But you must know you'll never get away with it."

9

For a moment there was silence, then softly from Welles came a small, soft chuckle. "Oh, yes I will," he said calmly and evenly, his self-confidence plain. "You'll see, Hedda, you'll see."

To the listening Hopper as he pronounced the words his assured tone dripped "arrogance," which she found infuriating ("Cockiness I can take; arrogance I abhor"). Again she warned him to expect trouble, and with a curt "goodbye!" she hung up.

Staring at the phone she hesitated. Then abruptly she picked it up, looked into her personal phone book, and put in a call to the Hearst lawyers. She could not have known it but that was exactly what the wily Mr. Welles expected and hoped she'd do.

2

Boy Wonder

The skyward-jutting central tower of the Chateau Marmont, Hollywood's most exclusive apartment hotel, rose high above the rushing, two-way traffic on Sunset Boulevard. Distant only minutes from all the major studios, the Marmont was a favorite of movie stars in transit or who temporarily lacked a home, as well as of producers, directors, writers, studio executives, and high-flyers in general. Into its quietly elegant, European-style lobby on July 21, 1939, walked the bearded, pipe-smoking Orson Welles, accompanied by two companions.

Stopping at the desk, each of the three filled out one of the distinctive little cards used by the Marmont in place of a register. After his name Welles entered his home address, 322 East 57 Street, New York City, then wrote in the date.

His checking in at the hotel caused little stir, but his arrival in town had not gone unnoticed. RKO's publicity staff had seen to that, starting with arranging to have a crowd of reporters on hand to greet him at the airport, with photographers snapping the obligatory picture of the smiling star ducking out through the plane's arched doorway. But for the RKO staff the task was an easy one since they were handling a pre-sold commodity, a *name,* and a big one. At that moment Orson Welles was the most famous young man in America.

Barely nine months before he stepped off the plane in Hollywood, he'd managed to rivet the attention of the whole country, frightening several million people with one of his regular weekly radio broadcasts. A realistic treatment of a tale called *The War of the Worlds* (first published in England in 1897), the story's locale was changed to the United States and was deceptively cast in the form of radio news bulletins. For many of those listening to the popular, one-hour show on WABC on the night of October 30, 1938, it seemed all too real. They had no doubt that an overwhelming force of invading Martians had landed in New Jersey and was fast overrunning the eastern half of the country.

Everywhere listeners were convinced that they were in immediate dire peril from the otherworldly marauders. In some places, the panic became concentrated, with mobs gathering and crowding for protection into police stations or army installations, or fleeing with

Welles' so-called "War of the Worlds" radio broadcast in 1938 made him famous while he was still short of his twenty-fifth birthday.

prized possessions into city streets or along deserted backcountry roads. In many towns and cities people wandered about in fright and confusion, begging for help.

Next day the story of the Martian scare was head-lined in every newspaper between New York and Los Angeles, all of them quoting the contrite apologies of the twenty-three-year-old Welles. It wasn't a hoax, he declared earnestly, hadn't been deliberate. There'd been no intention to fool anyone. The trouble, he pointed out, had started with those excitable listeners who had failed to pay attention during the broadcast (probably true to an extent, for several statements in the course of the drama did make it clear that the story was fiction, a fact that worked in Welles' favor when the inevitable lawsuits began to appear).

Interviewed for the newsreels that then played in all movie houses, his picture spread on front pages in every state, Welles' boldly handsome face and confi-dent bearing overnight became familiar sights to a fas-cinated public.

Without the Martian scare—and despite his prior successes in the theater and on radio—Welles' career would have taken a very different path. Certainly it would have been slower in developing, nor would it have been half so spectacular. Definitely it would not have included the triumph of *Citizen Kane,* not at least in its existing revolutionary form (he wouldn't have been given the chance). It was the immense publicity

generated around the dazzling Welles image by what
came to be called "The Man from Mars" broadcast,
that made him in the eyes of Hollywood so potentially
valuable an asset. Yet it wasn't all a matter of notoriety.
Hollywood's avid interest in the youthful showman
was sparked by the Mars incident, but only because it
was already aware of his remarkable rise in the New
York theater world.

During five packed years, first as a member of the
Federal Theater Project and then as cofounder and star
of a repertory group called the Mercury Players, he had
produced, directed, and taken the leading parts in several Broadway hits (a modern-dress *Julius Caesar,* Shaw's
Heartbreak House, and Dekker's *The Shoemaker's Holi-
day,* among them). He had also produced and directed
a sensational all-black *Macbeth.* On radio, also, the Mercury Players had become a fixture, again with Welles as
star.

As a result of all this national exposure, attention
in newspapers and big-time magazines had soon come
his way in abundance. Six months *before* the Martian
scare, in the spring of 1938, *Time* magazine had devoted
a cover story to him and his meteoric career. "Marvelous Boy," it was headed, and the lengthy, six-column
account made him indeed appear a phenomenon. As
director and star of *Julius Caesar,* commented *Time,*
Welles "made Brutus come alive in a blue-serge suit."
In *Heartbreak House,* again as director and star, playing
the part of the eighty-eight-year-old Captain Shotover,

he had "achieved a capital production of Shaw's notoriously wordy and difficult drama." Openly the magazine confessed its astonishment:

> If the career of the Mercury Theater . . . seems amazing, the career of Orson Welles, who this week is 23, is no less so. Were Welles' 23 years set forth in fiction form, any self-respecting critic would damn the story as too implausible for serious consideration. . . .
>
> Shadow to Shakespeare, Shoemaker to Shaw—all in one season, might be a whole career for most men, but for Welles is only a springboard to success. Nor does he want the Mercury to pin all its faith on the classics: he pines to do a real mystery, a real farce, a British pantomime, a fast revue, a Mozart opera. . . .
>
> The brightest moon that has risen over Broadway in years, Welles should feel at home in the sky, for the sky is the only limit that his ambitions recognize.

His photo on *Time*'s cover that same issue may have in a way been seen by Welles as a disappointment. Unrecognizable as the youthful star, it showed him in heavy makeup as the full-bearded, fierce-visaged octogenarian Captain Shotover.

Not surprisingly, it was as an actor that Welles first caught Hollywood's attention. During 1938 several offers reached him through his agent suggesting he play the leads in different films, *The Hunchback of Notre Dame,* for instance, or *Dr. Jekyll and Mr. Hyde.* All were turned down. The only arrangement that held interest for the supremely assured youth was one in which he enjoyed full control over a picture as producer-director-writer-star. It was, of course, an astonishing demand to be made by one so young and so wholly without experience in the art of filmmaking. He'd made one film short, a brief segment for use with a stage play, but that was all. About the making of a full-length feature film and the world of specialized knowledge that went into it, the infinite subtleties of camera technique and the particular problems of lighting and set arrangement it raised, he knew literally nothing.

Remarkably, in the spring of 1939, after extended negotiations with his agent, RKO met his terms. As he later recalled, while overjoyed, even he was more than a little surprised at getting all he desired, especially the part about exercising total control.

Early on the morning of July 22, the day after his arrival at the Marmont, Welles was driven to the RKO lot at Melrose and Gower Streets for the official contract signing. With him were the two men who'd accompanied him to Hollywood. One was John Houseman, co-founder of the Mercury and himself a producer-writer-director though not then an actor (years later he would fill the role of Professor Kingsfield in the popular television series *The Paper Chase*). The other man was Richard Baer, manager-personal assistant to Welles.

Driving through the tall iron gates of the RKO entrance, they were taken to the impressive offices of the studio's president, George Schaeffer, who welcomed them warmly. It was the fifty-year-old Schaeffer, then

RKO's president for barely a year, who had over the strong objections of studio skeptics pushed through the unusual arrangement with Welles. In great detail that arrangement was spelled out in the twenty-five-page document laid on the table by the smiling Schaeffer.

Two pictures were to be made. One must be completed by the end of that year—a deadline five months away!—the other could be ready any time during 1940. For both pictures Welles was to perform all four main functions: write, direct, produce, and take the starring role. Publicity was planned that would stress this one-man feat, emphasizing their new star's protean talents, all the more remarkable in view of his age.

Both the subjects and stories were to be chosen by Welles, and here RKO retained some slight authority, his choices needing studio approval. He could offer six ideas. If none was accepted, then RKO could suggest six of its own. If none on either side found favor the contract was canceled. For the first picture he'd be paid a fee of $65,000, plus 20 percent of the profits after recovery of all expenses. For the second he'd get $60,000, but his cut of the profits would rise to 25 percent.

The most important provision of all in Welles' view concerned the matter of control, in the casting as well as the making of both films. Once the final script had been approved by the studio he'd have a free hand. In particular the sets, as he promptly stipulated, were to be closed to outsiders. When shooting was in progress the set was to be his personal domain. Without his express permission no one was allowed to come visiting, not even studio executives. Aside from the fairly strict morals code then in force, no one at RKO could dictate any least item connected with the handling or development of the picture or its cast. At specific times he was obligated to show studio heads some of the daily rushes, but these he could himself pick and choose. Outside eyes would see only what he wanted them to see.

Regarding the most crucial item of all, the final cut, the last editing prior to the film's release, the arrangement was again unusual, Welles retaining full authority. The studio must accept his vision of the finished movie or nothing at all.

Aside from one or two instances involving long-established filmmakers (Charlie Chaplin most particularly), nothing quite like the Welles contract had been heard of in Hollywood before—certainly never where an untried newcomer was concerned. A triumph for Welles, the unique agreement eventually made possible *Citizen Kane*. Also, unfortunately, it would prove to be the beginning of Welles' own downfall.

In July 1939, however, as Welles happily signed his name and then shook hands with the delighted Schaeffer, both of those things were still a long way off.

❀

Around a large table in an RKO conference room sat a half-dozen men. Two female secretaries were also on hand, pencils poised over their notebooks. At the head of the table was George Schaeffer. Along one side were Welles and Houseman. The other men were RKO department chiefs. It was mid-August and the subject under discussion was Welles' projected first picture, a filming of Joseph Conrad's famous novelette of brooding evil in the jungle, *The Heart of Darkness*.

It was far from being an obvious choice as a first effort, a judgment loudly voiced by several well-informed if lesser voices at the studio. The Conrad story, they objected, while powerful and poetic in print, lacked the variety of incident needed to hold a viewing audience. "There's no use looking for a story here," insisted one opinion while pointing out the dearth of action, "in the screen sense of the word. This is not one of Conrad's best stories. He is wholly concerned here with building up a philosophical and mystical picture of a man who is a mystery to the reader even at the story's end."

This fairly evident flaw, the paucity of filmable incident, Welles himself had early recognized, but for what he had in mind it was actually an advantage. For him what counted was not the story itself. It was the technique, the method, the innovative approach he planned for turning it into a movie. Just coming up with another moneymaking picture of standard excellence, no matter how well received by the critics, didn't at all interest him. His reputation was for boldness and daring, for spectacular strokes, and for *Darkness* he had ready more than a few. The technique itself, *how* the story was told, would constitute the largest part of the picture's appeal, and the main element of that technique was a radically different use of the camera.

Conrad's lengthy, description-laden tale is not well-adapted for dialogue, for the intermingling of personalities. Told by a single narrator in long, set passages, the narration has little of the true ring of talk. The characters read and sound like what they are, carefully crafted literary compositions full of colorful detail.

Welles would soften their frequently stilted, run-on tone by making the camera itself the narrator—an old idea but little used, and which he planned to take well past its former limits. At no point would the narrator himself appear on the screen. The camera would be his eyes, and only his voice would be heard. The other characters would look at, react for, and play directly to the camera as they would to the narrator in person, or would go about their business in apparent ignorance of his (the camera's) presence.

In concept the idea was certainly intriguing and promising, even exciting. Whether it could be made to work on a sustained basis was another question, one that couldn't be answered until the picture was actually made, or most of it. That meant risking rather a lot of money at the outset. Still, in his confident way brushing aside all warnings, Welles had managed to gain Schaeffer's approval. The mid-August meeting had been called to set final plans for such things as budget, casting, set design, and production schedules. The script, written by Welles, also received its official OK at the meeting.

Fourteen weeks at most, the pipe-smoking, supremely relaxed young star assured the listening studio heads, would see the movie cast, rehearsed, shot, and in the can. That was less than four months, well under contract deadline. By year's end, he promised, his first movie would be on release throughout the country.

It wasn't mere youthful posturing. For nearly a month now, putting in fifteen- and eighteen-hour days, an old habit of his when under scheduling pressure, Welles had been a constant, busy presence at the RKO studios. Day after day, invading one department after another—wardrobe, makeup, editing, lighting, special effects, optics, the sound library, publicity, distribution—he impressed and amazed experienced technicians with his ready grasp of detail, his capacity for absorbing information. Constantly in his hand was a thick textbook or primer specially compiled by the studio for his personal use in which the whole range of moviemaking terminology was clearly set out, the many specialized functions and procedures explained (dissolve, jump cut, hanging miniature, iris in, iris out, pan shot, smear shot, and dozens of others). Particularly with the lighting, sound, and camera men he spent endless hours in eager discussion, handling the equipment itself until a big tripod camera or a heavy arc light took on a familiar feel.

But more than anything else his time was spent sitting, usually alone but sometimes accompanied by Houseman, in a darkened projection room watching movies. Shot by shot, scene by scene, he'd analyzed the images that flitted before his intensely concentrated gaze, often shouting up at the projectionist to halt a film so he could view a sequence over and over. Both American and foreign films were screened for him, but those he watched most were by director John Ford, two in particular: *The Informer,* made in 1935, and *Stagecoach,* released only weeks before and still playing around the country. *Stagecoach* he watched dozens of times, later openly declaring that "John Ford was my teacher and *Stagecoach* was my textbook."

Learning so much at so rapid a pace was a heady if exhausting experience and the process went on even as he began rehearsing the *Darkness* cast (all of them Mercury Theater players). It was after long hours of listening to the wonders to be heard in the RKO sound library that he blurted a remark which, intended or not, amusingly emphasized his own youth and inexperience, as well as his unique position in Hollywood. Waving his outstretched arms to include the whole sprawling studio complex, he exclaimed to a little knot of executives and technicians, "This is the biggest electric train set a boy ever had!" Quickly the comment found its way into the gossip columns, to be talked about and dissected by a town which still didn't know what to make of its latest stellar attraction.

Inevitable, and even in a way natural, was the movie colony's hesitant response to the Welles phenomenon, perfectly illustrated by a cynical remark that appeared

23

in *Daily Variety:* "A genius is a crackpot on a tightrope. Hollywood is watching Orson Welles, wondering if his foot will slip."

From some, the jealous and the insecure mostly, came resentment and rejection. From others, the curious and the confident, came a doubtful acknowledgment. From only a few, notably such directors as John Ford and King Vidor, came ready even warm acceptance. The child star Shirley Temple (at age eleven only a dozen years younger than Welles) played her own little studio-managed part in the welcoming game. When Welles early in August moved from the Marmont to a sumptuous rented estate in Hollywood's Brentwood section he became Shirley's next-door neighbor. A little past her prime but still a top box office draw, Shirley had Welles over for an afternoon's visit to face, not incidentally, a horde of reporters and photographers. Even the *New York Times* took note of the occasion, running a picture of the two stars together, the smiling Shirley sitting on a slide, the bearded Welles grinning beside her. On completion of the visit, said the *Times,* "he expressed himself as charmed by Miss Temple and her Mamma, and awed by the youngster's technique in handling news photographers."

Less friendly though not really malicious, as some have thought, was a bit of mocking verse that also made the papers. A take-off on Whitcomb Riley's popular poem *Little Orphan Annie,* it neatly hit Welles where he was most vulnerable, his now widely advertised all-embracing array of talents:

Little Orson Annie's
Come to our house to play
And josh the motion pitchurs up,
An' skeer the stars away,

An' shoo the Laughtons off the lot,
An' build the sets, and sweep,
An' wind the film, an' write the talk,
An' earn her board and keep.

An' all us other acters
When our pitchur work is done,
We set around the Derby bar
An' has the mostest fun

A-listenin' to the *me*-tales
That Annie tells about,
An' the Gobblewelles'll git YOU,
Ef you—Don't—Watch—Out!

Certainly Welles heard or read the mischievous lines as they made the rounds of the Hollywood studios and press. Whether he felt in them the "concentrated malice" suggested by one biographer is less likely. The widely quoted verse was, however, his first real experience of sustained public raillery against him personally. If he laughed along with everyone else, he must also have winced a little.

Helping a little to soothe away the hurt was an inquiry that reached him in August from the *Saturday Evening Post*, then America's leading popular magazine. They'd like to do a long article on him, explained the request, detailing his life and his career in the theater, an extended profile piece running in probably three consecutive issues (rare indulgence indeed). They knew how busy he was with his movie and his radio program, but if he agreed he'd have to spend considerable time talking with the writers. They wanted to start running the piece in January. Would Mr. Welles be interested?

He would.

Before the end of August *Heart of Darkness* was in full production and all was running smoothly. Eagerly awaited by the press, by Hollywood insiders, and by a goodly portion of the public was the name and subject of Welles' first film. Now RKO proudly announced it, at the same time handing out a sumptuous information brochure or press kit, "an elegant little folio containing portrait studies of Mr. Welles with a beard, approximately as he would appear in his forthcoming maiden production." In *Variety* a huge ad by RKO, trumpeting several of its upcoming pictures, crowed "Orson Welles . . . spectacular genius of the show world, brilliant actor and director, to make one picture a year . . . and what a picture is planned for his first!"

Time magazine, after duly reminding its readers that Welles had been "a holdout against Hollywood's blandishments for two years," revealed that for the new film Welles "would serve as actor, co-author, and director, and all without spending more than 18 weeks away from Broadway. First Picture—Joseph Conrad's *Heart of Darkness.*"

Readers of the newspapers in subsequent days were given a little more. Welles, explained one story, had grown his elegant beard expressly for his appearance in *Darkness,* but

> The announcement of the Conrad work was a little premature, for the copyright has not yet been cleared in the United States. . . . At any rate Welles is writing the scenario and he will appear in two roles in the film besides directing, producing, and editing it. For this RKO will pay him a reputed $100,000, and it is understood that the studio will exercise no supervision over the picture, merely footing the bill. Every one of the thousands of actors who have passed through Hollywood during the last quarter-century has striven to get the same kind of deal but no one else has succeeded.

No sooner had *Darkness* gotten underway, however, than it found itself facing difficulties. The first, not unexpectedly, arose from a prior contract Welles had signed with WABC radio back in New York City. Beginning the week of September 5, to honor his commitment for a weekly program—*The Campbell Playhouse,* sponsored by the Campbell Soup Company—he had to leave Hollywood and fly back to New York. For the next two months, out of each work week he'd have to give a total of three days to the Sunday night show in New York (part of Friday for travel, Saturday and Sunday for rehearsal and performance, part of Monday for the return flight to Hollywood, a journey at that time of some fifteen hours with a stop in Chicago). For

making *Darkness* he'd have only three full days each
week in Hollywood (Tuesday, Wednesday, Thursday),
along with parts of Monday and Friday. Not until mid-
November was he able to convince his radio sponsors
that originating the Playhouse in California was every
bit as "prestigious" as beaming it to the country from a
Broadway studio. By then he'd made ten weekly round-
trips back east and the *Darkness* schedule had inevitably suffered. The new arrangement reduced his radio
work to two days a week, much better for the film in
progress but still a decided handicap.

Now very doubtful appeared the December completion date for *Darkness*. They'd be lucky, all glumly
agreed, to have it by March 1940, skewing the planned
publicity campaign and upsetting the studio's schedule.

In drawing up Welles' RKO contract, Schaeffer had
been well aware of his new star's link to WABC and the
Campbell Playhouse, certainly knew about the heavy
demands it would make on his time and energy (it's not
clear whether he understood that it would originate in
New York rather than Los Angeles). But again Welles
had somehow made it all seem simple, this juggling of a
major film and a demanding weekly radio program, the
two tasks sited on opposite coasts. It was not the last
time he'd charm and insinuate his way into a corner.

The second difficulty came from a much more mo-
mentous event, the start of World War II in Europe.
On September 1, 1939, the long-simmering war scare at
last erupted when German troops invaded Poland.

Within days England and France honored their mutual assistance pacts with the beleaguered victim of Nazi aggression, and for the second time in a generation Europe was aflame. Two more years would pass before Pearl Harbor brought America into the conflict, but long before that the turmoil in the old world touched many aspects of American life, not least the Hollywood product.

Overseas markets for American movies had always bulked large in the profit picture of the major studios, often earning a third or more of net income. Now the two leading foreign markets, England and France, were drastically cut back as movie houses closed and a war mood settled on the populace. Attendance dropped nearly to half and it became very hard to predict the kinds of films that would find acceptance. Other important parts of the overseas market, Germany and Italy, for instance, before long were wholly shut off. *Time* magazine put the suddenly threatening situation succinctly: "The effect of war on shellshocked Hollywood last week was an incalculable crossfire of fears, dangers, hopes."

A shrinking market, in turn, made production budgets a prime concern, and to this new attitude *Darkness* was no exception. Already Welles' budget for the film had ballooned until it was approaching a million dollars, far in excess of the original estimate. At first, Schaeffer had gone along with the repeated increases urged by Welles as indispensable. Now, citing the war

29

and the loss of income, he insisted on drastic cuts being made, and Welles dutifully complied, or tried to. What finally killed the picture, in addition to financial concerns, was renewed doubt over the story's fitness for screen adaptation. Would the dense, brooding Conrad tale, no matter how cleverly innovative, have power to hold a mass audience caught up in its own daily concerns over life, death, and survival (Americans, too, though not yet directly threatened by the war, went in fear of what each new day might bring).

The answer, looming ever more obvious in the steady drumbeat of war news through September and October, was provided by Schaeffer and the RKO executive board. *Darkness* was canceled, and the cost to date—some $150,000—was written off.

Rather frantically, Welles began the search for a replacement. Literally dozens of ideas were studied by him and his staff without finding anything, and at one point he was ready to settle for a detective story with political overtones written by C. D. Lewis, *The Smiler with a Knife.* Some work was done on a script and on set design before the idea was abruptly scrapped as much too lightweight for a debut by the formidable Welles. Other possibilities were a bit likelier: *The Pickwick Papers, Jane Eyre, The Man Who Came to Dinner* (then running on Broadway, a role that Welles had earlier declined), *The Life of Machiavelli, The Life of Alexander Dumas,* an old novel called *The Fair God* by Lew Wallace, author of *Ben Hur.* Quite seriously he even thought of doing the story of the Borgias, with himself as Pope Alexander.

Nothing worked, nothing was able to satisfy both him and the studio bosses. As 1939 ended, after what had been a month's-long publicity flurry, the Welles bandwagon ground to an embarrassing dead stop.

Also sunk into disrepair at this time was Welles' personal life. His wife of five years, the former Virginia Nicholson, a New York socialite, had not come with him to California, remaining in the east with their only child, a little daughter. For some time the marriage had been in trouble, not helped by Welles' usual readiness to ignore his vows, and early in December lawyers for Virginia contacted him. "Mrs. Orson Welles to sue," headlined the *New York Times,* adding that she was leaving immediately for Reno, and that the two had already reached a property settlement. "Mrs. Welles and I do not feel that there is anything particularly new in this," commented Welles to the paper, not quite accurately. "We have been separated for a year." Trouble had been building between the two for a year, but no hint of it had reached the public until the news came that Mrs. Welles was Reno-bound.

Very soon the papers were also reporting the interesting fact that the beautiful Mexican actress Dolores Del Rio, who was at least ten years older than Welles, "had been seen frequently in recent months in his company."

Behind the closed doors of a private dining room at Chasen's Restaurant in Beverly Hills, eight men and one woman sat at a long table enjoying supper. Three bow-tied waiters periodically wheeled in carts laden with covered silver platters, then hovered round the table serving food, pouring wine, and clearing away spent dishes. The date was December 18, 1939. The occasion was an emergency meeting of the Mercury Players. Present were Welles, Houseman, Herb Drake, Baer, William Alland, Richard Wilson, Albert Schnei-der, and a secretary. Also on hand as an interested ob-server was RKO's George Schaeffer.

Despite the elegant surroundings the mood was not festive. Hints of more bad news had preceded the meeting indicating that cancellation of *Darkness* and the failure to replace it with another picture had created a financial crisis for the group, and at the meal's end Schaeffer made it official. On the last day of the year, he said, the studio would halt all salary payments to the Mercury and its staff including the half-dozen actors it had brought out from New York. Payments would re-sume only when a new picture had been approved and was actually in production.

Adamant that another film would soon be up and running, firm in his wish to keep the original *Darkness* cast from scattering, Welles gruffly announced that his entire Campbell Playhouse income would be used to pay salaries in the meantime. All during the several courses of the meal he'd been drinking steadily, and his mood was not pleasant. As one of the company recalled, "In preparation for this distasteful conversation he had absorbed more than his normal quantity of alcohol. His eyes were bloodshot, his face was clammy and white." Never a man to bother himself about finances, Welles was startled to hear Schneider say in response to the order to keep everyone on salary, "Orson, we can't. There isn't nearly enough and there won't be for a long time."

"What!"

"We don't have the money. You know we pulled down a lot in advance, and it's gone."

"What the hell have you done with it?" asked Welles, his deep voice suddenly angry and threatening. "You're supposed to manage the money. Where's it all gone?"

Schneider, staring his resentment, fell silent.

Turning to the others at the table, Welles growled, "I work myself to the bone for money, and you sons of bitches piss it away! Then you don't tell me! Not one of you—"

"Never mind about that, Orson," a voice interrupted dryly. "What do we do now about the cast? What *can* we do?"

Now on his feet, the glaring Welles swung around to face the questioner, Mercury cofounder John Houseman. It was a moment that all present had seen coming for months. Welles' growing fame and his tendency to take control of everything in sight had left Houseman in the shadows, his place with the Mercury ever more uncertain. As he later resentfully expressed it, his situation was "something between a hired, not too effective manager, a writer under contract, and an aging, not so benevolent relative." There was also more than a touch of plain jealousy on Houseman's part, expressed—to others, never to Welles—as a lament over the Mercury's supposed loss of artistic integrity. The loss was caused, as Houseman saw it, by the "publicity in unbelievable quantities" accorded the group's star. Welles, Houseman decided rather unreasonably, had sacrificed true creativity for the sake of publicity-generating "monkeyshines." During their time in Hollywood, with the pressures increased by the recurring demands of the Campbell Playhouse, moments of tension and outright disagreement between the two had not been rare.

"What would *you* do, my oh so wise friend?" asked Welles, his tone sharp, even bitter.

"Tell them the truth. For once tell your actors the truth!"

Welles exploded. "I don't lie to actors! I've never lied to an actor!" Breathing heavily he glowered at the defiant Houseman. "*You're* the one who lies. You're a crook and a cheat and everybody knows it. That's why they all distrust and hate you. . . ."

Seething yet managing to remain outwardly calm, Houseman stood up and made a show of neatly folding his napkin, then laying it down beside his plate. Without a word to anyone and without a backward glance he turned and walked away from the table. As he

Welles pays a publicity call on his Brentwood neighbor, child star Shirley Temple. The photo appeared in the *New York Times* on August 20, 1939, a month after he arrived in Hollywood.

neared the exit door a small object flew past his head, smashed against the wall nearby, and fell to the plush carpet. It was one of the sterno heating cans used at the tables to keep food warm. Infuriated by his colleague's silent departure, Welles had snatched it up and hurled it after him. As Houseman pulled the door open a second sterno can hit the wall (he'd been careful both times, Welles later claimed, to aim wide of the target).

Three days later a letter arrived at Welles' Brentwood home. It was from Houseman. He was quitting. "We have been through too much together and have had too much excitement and too much joy for me to let our partnership follow the descending curve of misunderstanding and mutual dissatisfaction . . . what happened the other night merely brought to a head a situation I have seen growing worse for some time." He was leaving Hollywood for good, he ended. He was going back to New York.

A few days after the unpleasantness at Chasen's the *Hollywood Reporter* weighed in with its estimate of the situation between Welles and the studio. "They are laying bets over on the RKO lot that the Orson Welles deal will end up without Orson ever doing a picture there," it smugly declared, echoing the town's insider talk. "The whole thing seems to be so mixed up no one can unravel it."

In his brief, meteoric career—barely seven years since his first appearance at age sixteen on a professional stage—Welles had known moments of disappointment, even comparative failure. This was different. Now he enjoyed full-fledged celebrity status, and here he was in the national spotlight facing massive professional disaster. With the appearance in January 1940 of the lengthy *Saturday Evening Post* article the point was cruelly sharpened. While much high praise for his past accomplishments was spread through the three installments, for the shaken Welles one paragraph in particular would have stood out:

> There are different estimates of Welles. One school regards him as the most important influence in the theatre today; another regards him as an upstart with a wonderful bag of tricks. As an actor he has been called everything from "a whining sea cow" to a coming Richard Mansfield. Some of his admirers think he has scattered himself over so many departments of human activity that he is not likely to achieve first rank in any of them.

3

Aging Wonder

For a private office it was beyond anything most people would ever see, a large, impossibly luxurious room:

High, barrel-vaulted ceiling with ribbed rafters that swept up from floor level in long, graceful curves—wall paneling of costly woods, all studded with golden bas-relief figures—furniture of massive design, made of richly carved woods, upholstered in silk or damask—a profusion of Old Master paintings and medieval tapestries—dozens of screened bookcases holding thousands of richly bound books including rare first editions—heavy, cut-glass chandeliers of unique cylindrical design—thick-piled rugs and carpets covering the teak floor.

The room occupied one whole corner of the third floor in the main building of California's grandest, most impressive private estate. Situated on the Pacific coast about halfway between Los Angeles and San Francisco, known as San Simeon, the name of the nearest town, it was an agglomeration of specially designed structures erected during some twenty years at a cost of untold millions of dollars. Set atop a private mountain in the midst of a quarter-million-acre private preserve, the huge and ornate dwellings offered residents and their guests every comfort, convenience, luxury, and indulgence conceivable. Aside from the several buildings, a fully stocked zoo was its most striking feature (lions, leopards, zebras, elephants, eagles, emus, bison, giraffe, antelope only begin the list).

At this moment, ten o'clock on the morning of July 22, 1939, the office was occupied by one man, a bulky, long-faced, thin-nosed individual dressed in a light gray checkered suit and a bright tie. Near the room's center he sat hunched over a long oaken table laden with files and papers. Telephone in hand he was speaking, as he did every morning, with the editor of one of the many newspapers he owned.

At one side of the room, spread in neat rows on a wide expanse of rug, were some twenty newspapers, all with full front pages showing.

The phone conversation was a lengthy one, with the editor at the other end doing most of the listening. Finished talking at last, the man dropped the old-style phone back onto its spindly cradle, rose from his chair and walked over to the newspaper display. There for the next half-hour he stood eyeing the large scare headlines blaring from paper after paper, comparing them for content and effectiveness.

The several photographs on each page earned his particular attention, illustrations in his estimate being of equal or greater value in a newspaper than words. One picture showed a United Airlines plane at Los Angeles airport with a tall, smiling, dark-haired young man ducking out through the arched doorway to be greeted by a trim, uniformed hostess. This photo the man especially noted, for one of his habits was to be aware of the comings and goings of famous and influential people, and this new arrival was famous indeed. His name—announced by the caption as Orson Welles—Hearst certainly had heard before, if only when spoken by his friends and colleagues in movie and newspaper circles.

Lingering a moment on the photo of Hollywood's newest luminary, he made a mental note to add the youthful star's name to the San Simeon guest list. Celebrities of all sorts were a staple on the fabulous mountain-top, paying visits of days or weeks. Just then, William Randolph Hearst was well aware, there was no celebrity whom more people wished to meet than the wonder boy from New York.

After fifty years on the American scene, a half-century of intense social, political, and personal embroilment, by 1939 Hearst had become overlord of a vast communications empire, one wielding immense power and influence. Included were twenty-nine newspapers, a dozen leading magazines, an international news service, radio stations in most major population areas, and an established movie studio, to mention only his leading properties.

Son of a multi-millionaire father, himself now far richer, Hearst began his career in 1887 as owner-publisher of the *San Francisco Examiner,* a gift from his father. Twenty-four years old and just expelled from Harvard, he soon turned the respected old journal from legitimate reporting to a career of sensationalism. Solely for the sake of circulation he adopted and improved on every low trick and technique of the day's "yellow journalism." A frothy blend of exaggeration, distortion, excess, and outright fakery became the *Examiner*'s hallmark—scandal, pseudo-science, disasters, an undercurrent of sexual innuendo, all wrapped in a variety of noisy "crusades" on behalf of a vague entity called "the people."

Before long the *New York Journal,* bought for him by his indulgent mother, came under his control, and the same cynical formula was employed. Rapidly then, other papers were acquired, Hearst soon possessing a long string of them, making one of the country's first true "chains." Promptly as each new paper was grabbed it was revamped to fit the degraded *Examiner* model. It was Hearst, more than any other man, who introduced plain vulgarity into American journalism, disguising it with an occasional softer, soberer tone, a mixture that made a great appeal to the immature and the unschooled. Knowingly, deliberately, he set out to corrupt the traditional American newspaper, and he succeeded.

"Regular readers of a Hearst paper," wrote one of his more sympathetic biographers, "would find other newspapers insipid, destitute of the racy detail to which they were accustomed. Conversely, a reader of the sedate *New York Times* on turning to a Hearst sheet would be apt to shudder at the discovery of a frantic world he had not dreamed existed."

The comment is typical of much that has more recently been written of Hearst following a trend toward veiling his culpability, close to but not quite the truth. It slights the relevant fact that the so-called "racy detail" almost always consisted of deliberate distortion, a blithe wrenching of prosaic reality, twisting and heightening it for maximum dramatic effect. All too often that same detail was wholly invented. Misleading also is the odd phrase "frantic world," much too mild for the subtly pandering, lying, tasteless mixture that was the Hearstian formula.

What was said of Hearst in 1906 by Theodore Roosevelt was no exaggeration: "He preaches the gospel of envy, hatred, and unrest. . . . He cares nothing for the nation nor for any citizen in it. . . . He is the most potent single influence for evil we have in our life." Thirty-three years later *Time* magazine precisely echoed those damning words: "No other press lord wielded his power with less sense of responsibility; no other press matched the Hearst press for flamboyance, perversity, and incitement of man's hysteria. . . . His appeal was not to men's minds but to those infantile emotions which he never conquered in himself; arrogance, hatred, frustration, fear."

In many ways over and over Hearst proved the accuracy of that opinion, perhaps never more clearly or blatantly than in his open and strong support of Hitler and Mussolini in the years leading up to World War II. Both dictators he repeatedly praised in editorials, both he paid handsomely for contributing regular unedited articles to his papers.

Examples of his baleful influence make a long, sorry list. Rightly he is blamed for his part in bringing on the Spanish-American War over Cuba in 1898, the hysteria created by his newspapers—based on sensational exaggeration and massive deliberate lying—helping mightily to stampede the public into acceptance of that short, bloody conflict. Most chilling of all was his role in the assassination of President McKinley in 1901, a role which earned him fierce public condemnation, and from which he recovered only with great difficulty. Always a bitter opponent of McKinley, editorials in Hearst papers against the president and his policies grew increasingly savage in tone until they actually encouraged the idea of assassination. "If bad institutions and bad men cannot be got rid of except by killing," counseled an editorial in the *New York Evening Journal* on McKinley's reelection, "then the killing must be done."

Stories that in the pocket, or the house or effects, of the captured assassin was found a copy of that inflammatory editorial were rife at the time. They have never been proved or disproved.

At age forty Hearst married for the first time, choosing as his bride a Broadway showgirl. After some dozen years and the birth of five sons, he took a mistress, also a Broadway chorus girl, this one thirty-five years his junior. A perky blond named Marion Davies, she was an uncomplicated, not-quite-pretty young woman with lofty stage ambitions, but little real talent. She could dance a little, act a little, sing a little, deliver a line of dialogue more or less ably. Eventually she might have become a dependable supporting actress, but she was utterly unable to "fill" a true leading role and was devoid of any star quality. Despite that, the enamored Hearst proceeded to give her leading parts in a series of pictures he made at his Cosmopolitan Studios (silents first, then talkies). The power of the press—his press—he counted on to force her acceptance by the movie-going public, as he had forced the Spanish-American War on that same public. A strong supporting cast and over-lavish spending on production values did the rest, and to a limited extent it worked.

Each of the Davies pictures was greeted by the Hearst chain of papers and magazines with a blizzard of outrageous praise ("Miss Davies Hailed as One of the Greatest Artists on the Screen," shamelessly lied one headline). The public, accustomed to believing what it read in the papers, or a goodly portion of it, accepted the lies as sober, legitimate film criticism. In time, however, rumors of Hearst's trickery and word-of-mouth criticism caught up with the imposture. Most of Davies' nearly fifty films (thirty silents, sixteen talkies made during twenty years) lost money.

Her last picture—*Ever Since Eve,* costarring Robert Montgomery and featuring a trio of first-rate professionals, Patsy Kelly, Frank McHugh, and Allen Jenkins—was released in the summer of 1937. It flopped, not least because of comments like this from the *New York Times:* "After playing the eye-batting ingenue for more years than it would be polite to mention, Miss Davies apparently feels she has mastered the role sufficiently to begin her cycle all over again."

To her credit, the mature Marion Davies, looking back, readily confessed the truth. "When I was young I just lived for the stage," she explained shortly after Hearst's death in 1951. "I even hated my own home because it wasn't glamorous. I thought, like every poor idiot does, that I had a career." The idea that she might marry and raise a family, she admitted, never entered her mind: "If only I had stopped to realize how stupid I was. I had no talent for the theater. I had no talent, period. I had the ambition that my life was made for a

Top right: Spurious praise for Marion Davies' acting talents in a Hearst newspaper, the *New York American,* on August 5, 1923. Readers weren't fooled.

Bottom right: Young Marion Davies in a publicity shot for an early movie.

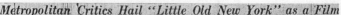

Metropolitan Critics Hail "Little Old New York" as a Film

MARION DAVIES ACCLAIMED AS GREAT ARTIST

"Theatre, Star, Picture, Direction, All Call for Superlatives," Says S. Fay Kaufman in Evening Telegram.

STAGE VERSION ECLIPSED

"Heroine's Role Couldn't Be in Better Hands," Says Sun and Globe; "Lives the Part," Evening Mail.

Supplementing the Metropolitan morning newspapers in their sustained praise of the great Cosmopolitan film spectacle, "Little Old New York," and of the rare qualities of the work of the star, Marion Davies, the reviewers of the evening newspapers continued in proclaiming the new offering a great triumph.

The reviewer of the New newspapers, which occupied attacked to new Cosmopolitan Theatre, Columbus Circle, yesterday under governor's interested that the production in craftsmen Joseph Urban, was attuned to a reference to fine first night audiences.

Notice has there been expressed by the critics such unanimity of approval of a film as that accorded "Little Old New York."

Following are extracts from the comments of the evening newspaper reviewers:

S. J. KAUFMAN in the Evening Telegram.—Theatre, star, picture and direction they all call for superlatives ...

REMARKABLE PORTRAYAL OF A CENTURY AGO

BOWLING GREEN in 1807 has been faithfully reproduced in the newest Cosmopolitan production, "Little Old New York," starring Marion Davies, that last Wednesday night opened the new Cosmopolitan Theatre on Columbus Circle. Many of the most interesting episodes of this great historical film are laid on the streets of lower Manhattan in the early days of the nineteenth century, and to reproduce Bowling Green in its entirety the largest armory in New York City was used as a motion picture studio. More than four hundred persons took part in the famous whipping-post scene, when Patricia O'Day, masquerading as a boy, breaks up a prize fight by calling out the fire department on a false alarm and is taken to the village whipping post for punishment. Marion Davies in "Little Old New York" has settled down for a long run at the newest of Broadway cinema palaces. Victor Herbert and his orchestra play at both performances daily.

Miss Davies Called 'One of Best Actresses' and 'One of Greatest Artists on Screen'

WHAT the critics of the leading New York morning newspapers think of Miss Marion Davies's triumph in "Little Old New York," the magnificent Film play of the early days of the metropolis, is indicated by the following brief extracts from their notices:

HARRIETTE UNDERHILL, NEW YORK TRIBUNE.—It is doubtful if Miss Davies ever dreamed that she would become one of the best ... and a fine achievement for the director, Sidney Olcott. The Park emerges as perhaps the heaviest theatre in this highly theatrical borough.

MISS DAVIES IMPRESSES

career and I was never going to leave the stage. But I had no talent even for pictures, just a little tap dancing. . . . I didn't make the grade myself, I was pushed. If I hadn't been pushed I would have gotten a job selling gloves at a counter. I wouldn't have been happy doing that."

When she uttered those painfully honest words she was quietly lamenting her thirty-year commitment to Hearst, which had kept her from marriage and a family of her own. To live as the pampered toy of one of the world's richest men had been a situation too tempting to refuse. By then she could well afford to feel sorrow and regret over a life virtually thrown away. Through the generosity of Hearst she had become an extremely wealthy woman. Unfortunately she had also become and had long been known as a confirmed alcoholic.

For a time in the early part of the twentieth century politics had also claimed Hearst's rapt attention. Suffering the delusion that often grips those who wield great power in the public arena, he seriously saw himself occupying the White House, and in 1904 he began his campaign by winning (buying) a seat in Congress. But he failed to get much beyond that, all his frantic subsequent efforts missing badly. A try for mayor of New York City in 1905 went wildly awry, as also for governor of the same state two years later. With that he gave up, content to see himself and his newspapers as a power behind the throne in Democratic circles.

Eccentric in his tastes, endlessly self-gratifying, with nearly unlimited millions at his disposal, he became a

collector of art and antiques on a grand scale. So constantly, so hugely did he spend on his passion, here and
in Europe, that he finally needed entire warehouses, in
California and New York, to hold the overflow from
his various estates. The statuary, paintings, tapestries,
and *objets d'art* of all sorts came in so steadily and so
rapidly that there wasn't always time to unpack or display them. Many items remained in their crates for
years, and even well after Hearst's death.

Here, if anywhere, in his frantic, headlong pursuits
as a mere indiscriminate *collector* (*what* was collected
hardly mattered), is revealed the mental and emotional
instability that underlay all Heart's actions, public and
private. The outward impression of normalcy he gave
to most of those he met in the course of an ordinary
day was woefully misleading. In reality, in his apparently normal daily behavior he made decisions about
his business and personal affairs which spoke, subtly
or loudly to those able to read them, of his aberrant
outlook.

Hearst was a man flawed at the core, a creature of
his own fabulous inherited wealth, which led him to
believe that *anything* could be bought. Of course, in
that belief he was in a way not far wrong. It was
money and his willingness to spend it without stint
that gave him what, personally, he wanted most: a
world of his own, physically set apart, a magnificent,
unequaled world able to draw to itself, as a veiled form
of homage to its master, the famous and accomplished
people of the earth.

This he had at San Simeon, with its fifty miles of ocean frontage, its enchanted castle on a hill, and its unending flow of celebrity guests—actors, actresses, artists, statesmen, writers, politicians, journalists, scientists, philosophers, critics, columnists, European royalty. Sumptuous daily meals served by liveried waiters at a long table in a cathedral-like dining room were the rule. Lavish costume parties lasting for days were not unusual, the costumes being supplied to all fifty or sixty guests by Hearst, with a crowd of seamstresses and tailors on hand to do the fitting. Picnics that called for transport of the guests by twenty or thirty limousines to a tent-covered beach serving gourmet meals were frequent.

Not even the Medicis in medieval Italy had achieved such an astonishingly opulent, all-encompassing display of conspicuous grandeur, artificial and vulgar as it was.

He was tall and painfully thin. Bespectacled, with dark, unruly hair, his pinched expression bespoke the intellectual. In the back of the chauffeured limousine sent for him by Hearst he sat staring at the passing orange groves. Then all at once far in the distance through a gap between two groves he saw what he thought "a most surprising sight."

Like an island off a cliff-bound coast, as he later described it, a rocky hill rose abruptly. On its summit "in a kind of stony efflorescence, stood a castle. But what a castle! The donjon was like a skyscraper, the bastions plunged headlong with the effortless swoop of concrete dams. The thing was Gothic, medieval, baronial." Through the elaborate main entrance gate some minutes later rolled the limousine, starting the five-mile drive up to the twin-towered main house, La Casa Grande, as it was called.

Going along the winding road the man in the limousine was startled to see, loudly chattering among a scatter of rocks behind wire fencing, a large group of baboons. As the car drove past, every one of the hairy, long-snouted animals fell silent, staring in curiosity at the moving vehicle.

Pulling up before the lofty sculptured main entrance of La Casa Grande—a tall, gated portal with the air of an old Spanish church—the limousine glided to a halt. Quickly the chauffeur got out and hurried around to open the door for his passenger. Brushing back his hair with a hand and adjusting his glasses, out stepped one of the day's most famous, most respected novelists, the Englishman Aldous Huxley, aged forty-three. It is September 1937, and the Huxley writings are much talked about, not only in literary circles: *Antic Hay, Point Counter Point, Brave New World, Eyeless in Gaza.*

Only weeks before, Huxley with his wife had arrived in America hoping to find lucrative work as a scriptwriter (he caught on with MGM), and Hearst had lost no time in adding him to his celebrity collection. This once, however, he blundered badly in choosing his guests, of course unknowingly. Within a matter of months, after several more visits to the enchanted castle, Huxley would begin a new novel. San Simeon and Hearst himself would be its subject—*target* would be a better word, for the book would not be at all kind to the unwary host.

Concerning the first meeting between the two men on this initial visit no actual detail has survived. But in his novel Huxley gives a passage which evidently reflects his first sustained contact with both Hearst and his mistress, an incident which took place at the magnificent heated outdoor swimming pool (the Neptune Pool, made of white and antique-green marble, and surrounded by pillars, statues, and porches).

The scene opens with Jeremy Pordage (Huxley) in the water floating serenely on his back, and Jo Stoyte (Hearst, aged seventy-three) in bathing trunks sitting on a poolside couch. Virginia Maunciple (Marion Davies, aged thirty-nine) in a white swimsuit is standing at a bar, glass in hand. She takes another sip, puts down the glass and climbs to the diving platform, plunges in, and comes up under the floating Pordage. Catching him by the belt, she pulls him under:

> "You asked for it," she said, as he came up again, gasping and spluttering, to the surface. "Lying there without moving, like a silly old Buddha." She smiled at him with an entirely good-natured contempt. . . .

50

She turned, swam to the ladder, climbed out, walked to the table on which the bottles and glasses were standing, drank the rest of her whisky and soda, then went and sat down on the edge of the couch on which, in black spectacles and bathing drawers, Mr. Stoyte was taking his sun bath.

"Well, Uncle Jo," she said in a tone of affectionate playfulness, "feeling kind of good?"

"Feeling fine, baby," he answered . . . and laid a square, thick-fingered hand on the young woman's bare knee.

Through half-closed eyelids, Miss Maunciple gave him a secret and somehow indecent look of understanding and complicity; then uttered a little laugh and stretched her arms. "Doesn't the sun feel good!" she said; and, closing her lids completely, she lowered her raised arms, clasped her hands behind her neck and threw back her shoulders. It was a pose that lifted the breasts, that emphasized the inward curve of the loins and the contrary swell of the buttocks. . . .

Through his dark glasses, Mr. Stoyte looked up at her with an expression of possessiveness at once gluttonous and paternal. Virginia was his baby, not only figuratively and colloquially, but also in the literal sense of the word. His sentiments were simultaneously those of the purest father-love and the most violent eroticism. . . .

Mr. Stoyte's regard travelled up to the auburn hair and came down by way of the rounded forehead, of the wide-set eyes, and small, straight, impudent nose to the mouth. That mouth—it was her most striking feature. For it was to the mouth's short upper lip that Virginia's face owed its characteristic expression of child-like innocence. . . .

Delicious creature! The hand that had lain inert, hitherto, upon her knee slowly contracted. Between the broad spatulate thumb and the strong fingers, what smoothness, what a sumptuous and substantial resilience!

Huxley finishes the passage by showing himself so embarrassed by what he saw of the intimate poolside tableau that he climbed quickly out of the water and hurried off.

In writing his novel on Hearst, Huxley didn't rely for information entirely on his own observation at San Simeon or on the inevitable gossip he picked up among the Hollywood crowd. Only the year before his arrival in the movie capital there had appeared two book-length biographical studies of Hearst's checkered fifty-year saga, both claiming to tell all. On the evidence of the texts, Huxley made good use of both volumes, of course for his own creative purposes disguising and transforming what he took.

The first of the two books, *Imperial Hearst: A Social Biography,* by Ferdinand Lundberg, appeared in March 1936 with a preface by famed historian Charles Beard. Announced as "the only complete exposition" of the Hearst career, it pointedly avoided discussing the private life. Beard in his preface, however, paused long enough to observe that when the publisher's race was finally run, "He will depart loved by few, and respected by none whose respect is worthy of respect. When the cold sneer of command at last fades from his face, none will be found to honor his memory. . . . This is not to say that Hearst possesses no virtues. Nero and Caligula had virtues."

In a fully documented narrative, Lundberg set out in graphic detail every corrupt, deceptive, and unworthy action of significance committed by Hearst and his newspapers, beginning with the hectic *San Francisco Examiner* days. In addition to the many incidents of fakery and distortion already on the record, the charges included forgery, outright theft of public documents, and subtle financial blackmail of advertisers. After almost four hundred scathing pages, Lundberg sums up:

> William Randolph Hearst's career has required the continuous deception of the American people. . . . Down through the years he had played a great and ghastly part in shaping the American mind . . . not because he has become the voice of the people but because adequate, widespread, and popularized criticism of his career has been lacking. . . .
>
> The very elements in our society which should have been busy exposing him have been silent because, in either close or distant ramifications, they profited by being silent. . . . Without the support of bankers and industrialists for his irresponsible antisocial rampages he would be merely a senile clown.

The second Hearst biography to appear in 1936 was published a month after the first: *Hearst: Lord of San*

Simeon, by Oliver Carlson and Ernest Bates. While treating their subject's public life candidly and in full, the two also made up for Lundberg's neglect of more personal things. Inevitably, the spotlight fell on his extramarital proclivities. "His flaunting in the face of the public," wrote Carlson/Bates, "his personal disregard for accepted convention is doubtless merely a phase of his psychic compulsion to feel himself an exception to all the rules. At the same time, his habit of delving into divorce-court scandals and backstairs gossip against his enemies, while believing that his wealth protected him against similar attacks, would almost excuse a biographer in over-emphasizing the whole subject."

Miss Davies came along, the book explained, at just the right moment in Hearst's life, when he needed "a new interest . . . to divert his thoughts" from his failure in politics and on the international stage. "His successful flouting of public opinion by the openness of his relations with the beautiful actress enabled him to feel that he was an exception to the ordinary rules made for lesser men." Miss Davies' real name was Marion Douras, the book went on. She was born in Brooklyn, New York, the daughter of a minor local politician. In 1916 the fifteen-year-old hopeful landed a spot in the chorus of the hit Ziegfeld musical *Chu Chin Chow*. At the theater one night Hearst spotted her, took her to his personal hideaway apartment in the city, and proceeded to promote her film career. "Not only is she the only star of Hearst's Cosmopolitan Corporation," wrote Carlson/Bates, "she is also its president with a salary of $104,000 a year."

Listing Miss Davies' better-known films with titles and dates, Carlson/Bates stated frankly that, simultaneously with the appearance of Davies' first films, the motion-picture editors of Hearst papers across the country suddenly and with great enthusiasm "discovered" the newcomer. Loudly they hailed her as the "find" of the year and she was "photographed and interviewed almost endlessly. . . . In every instance the Hearst press gushed forth enormous praise, but other papers were not overly enthusiastic, nor was the audience response any too gratifying."

Coming to the amazing fact of San Simeon, and Hearst's role as "Lord" of it, Carlson/Bates conceded the sheer magnificence of it all, yet unlike many who saw and wrote of the marvel, still managed to place it nicely in context: "With the power that moves mountains, which is not faith but wealth, he has raised, as with the touch of some mad enchanter's wand, a castle that looks like a Spanish mission with a dining hall that looks like a monk's refectory, 'cottages' that look like châteaux, everything looking like something else than what it is except the flying field, tennis courts, and swimming pools, which themselves have an unreal air on this aloof hilltop, set cheek-by-jowl with so many relics and imitations of medievalism."

As a collector of art and antique statuary Hearst is made by the two biographers to seem exactly what he

Hearst's fantastic "Castle on a Hill" at San Simeon on the California coast.

Hearst with guests in the elaborate dining hall at San Simeon, "the Refectory," as it was called.

was, weirdly eccentric, if not actually unbalanced. He possessed the country's finest collections of armor, stained glass, old silver, gothic mantelpieces, old furniture, and Mexican saddles. Not far behind were his collections of pottery, tapestries, costumes, and paintings (his most valued painting, an ancient Madonna, "hangs in Miss Davies' bedroom").

Stored at San Simeon or displayed were such rarities as worm-eaten choir stalls from Europe, old marble fireplaces, whole ceilings from a French castle, mummies from Egypt, and the actual bed used by Cardinal Richelieu. "He has collected—the Lord knows what he hasn't collected! Loot from all the world is gathered at San Simeon."

Carlson/Bates end their book by picturing the elderly Hearst, while his guests mingle happily in a room apart from him, "with stooped shoulders and sagging cheeks, seated somewhere in a corner." What he now fears most, they emphasize, is not loneliness or neglect, it is death and what comes afterward: "The unmentioned and unmentionable word booms through San Simeon louder than the hubbub of all its coming and departing guests. . . . Never dare to mention Death in his presence."

❀

Huxley's novel—ponderously titled *After Many a Summer Dies the Swan,* a line from Tennyson's *Tithonus*— was not written as a simple *roman à clef* or merely to create a sensation. He used it or tried to use it as a means of saying something on larger issues, on the abuse of power, on what he considered the foolish desire for immortality, on the insanity of war—he was a pacifist and Europe at that moment was fast heating up—or the problem of the human soul when sunk in an ethical dilemma (the book's focus is none too sharp). Still, it was plainly and inescapably modeled on the extravagant Hearst career and personality, and the staggering fact of San Simeon. Its plot makes extensive use, for instance, of a notorious incident in Hearst's life of fifteen years before, one that might have been the basis for a movie script. Involved were the Hearst yacht, the seduction of Marion Davies, and the sudden death of a prominent film producer, Thomas Ince. As detailed by Carlson/Bates, and by others then and afterwards, the story is left without a proper denouement. It went like this:

On November 19, 1924, most newspapers announced the death of the forty-three-year-old Ince, giving the cause as heart failure, induced by an acute attack of indigestion. He'd been stricken, it was said, on a train while returning to Los Angeles from San Diego. Gradually over the next few days further information came out. The illness had occurred not on a train but aboard "a yacht" in the waters off San Diego. Then it was revealed that the yacht was Hearst's own resplendent boat *Oneida*. A large party had been aboard, it was explained, including film comedian Charlie Chaplin.

With that the rumors started flying, for Chaplin's pursuit of Marion Davies had, well prior to the Ince affair, found a voice in the gossip columns, also supplying hints that the lady was not above having a quiet fling on the side.

The whispered story that finally took shape depended on the fact that Ince and Chaplin bore a close facial and physical resemblance to each other.

Aboard the *Oneida* one night, ran the fast-unfolding tale, Hearst had missed Marion from the crowd of guests milling in the boat's main salon. He went to his cabin for a pistol, then looked around the several darkened decks and knocked on doors. Suddenly he came on Miss Davies in a dimly lit cabin, in what seemed a compromising situation with a man whom in the half-light he took to be Chaplin. Enraged, from his pocket he pulled the pistol and shot the man, only to discover that it was not Chaplin. It was producer Ince.

A massive cover-up ensued, it was said, in which all on board were sworn to secrecy—or threatened, or paid for their silence. After a flurry of public interest, and some initial police involvement, the story somehow faded from the papers, and eventually, for most, from public awareness. After a year or so it survived only as gossip at Hollywood's insider parties. Since then Hearst's biographers have given the story little credence, noticing it only in passing. Few now take it seriously, though there has never been a sustained investigation.

In the Huxley novel the Ince story, slightly altered, forms the climax. The setting is transferred from the confined stage of the Hearst yacht to the more gorgeous setting of San Simeon, by the side of the Neptune pool one dusky evening. The Hearst character, named Jo Stoyte, accidentally comes on the Davies character, named Virginia Maunciple, in mild dalliance on a couch beside the pool with the Chaplin character, named Dr. Obispo (San Simeon house physician). Furious, but undetected by the two, he rushes off to get a pistol he keeps in his room. While he's gone, Obispo leaves to fetch a comb for Virginia and is replaced on the couch by another man, the Ince character, Stoyte's personal assistant, Peter Boone.

Beside the languid, bathing-suited Virginia, Boone sits down to talk, when darting out from behind a marble pillar comes Stoyte, wildly firing the pistol. As Boone falls, Stoyte is stunned to discover his mistake, and at that juncture Obispo returns to find Virginia hysterical and Stoyte down on his knees, "trying, with a pocket handkerchief, to staunch the blood that was still pouring out of the two wounds, one clean and small, the other cavernous, which the bullet had made as it passed through Pete's head."

Promptly Obispo sizes up the situation, quietly pockets the discarded gun, then proceeds with a few well-chosen comments to reel in the shattered millionaire. Stoyte in his panic forgets that he is speaking to the man he tried to kill, and begs for his help. "I'll make it worth your while," he pleads. "You can have anything you care to ask for." Obispo's reply is a cool, "Now you're talking turkey."

All the essential details of the Ince affair are in place in the Huxley book, and couldn't be missed by a knowledgeable reader. Then the novel ends with another recognizable Hearst touch, an extended satirical treatment of his widely rumored terror of death, and his pathetic efforts to find a way of prolonging his life indefinitely. Stoyte goes to England to meet a man, a member of the royalty, who supposedly has found such a method (a diet of raw carp gut) and who has already survived for over two hundred years. Meeting the man, he's appalled to encounter a misshapen, apish caricature of a human.

The writing of the lengthy novel, well over a hundred thousand words, had taken nearly a year, and a month or so after its completion the Huxleys to celebrate threw a party. At their home overlooking Santa Monica—*Time* called it "their secluded wooden cottage in Pacific Palisades"—on the afternoon of July 30, 1939, a small but select group assembled. Present among others were several film stars, Helen Hayes, Paulette Goddard, Lillian Gish, Greta Garbo, and Charlie Chaplin, who to the delight of the company performed his balloon-dance from *The Great Dictator*, just then shooting.

Arriving late by cab from the Chateau Marmont was another guest with movie connections, the much-talked-of Orson Welles. In town only nine days, still settling in at RKO, he was a very busy man, putting in long days of study and research at the studio getting ready to do *Heart of Darkness*. But he couldn't pass up Huxley's invitation, unexpected as it was, bringing the first real gesture of friendship he'd had from the Hollywood establishment. Huxley, as it turned out, was as intrigued by Welles as Welles was impressed to meet the famous novelist. In the course of the afternoon the two celebrated artists went off by themselves and spent a pleasant half-hour in rambling chat. The new novel of course came in for a good share of comment, with Welles showing considerable interest in its link to Hearst, especially by way of the Ince affair.

4

Conjuring *Kane*

A sleek new Buick convertible, top down, sped along U.S. Highway 15, heading east out of Los Angeles. Three hundred miles away was its first overnight stop on the six-day trip cross-country to New York City: Las Vegas, just over the Nevada border. It was the morning of September 8, 1939.

At the wheel was a young aspiring screenwriter named Tom Phipps. In the seat beside him sat a fellow screenwriter, this one a veteran possessing long and intimate experience of Hollywood. A friendly, talkative, bluff-faced man, his name was Herman Mankiewicz. To movie people, studio executives and many of the stars, he was known simply as Mank. At this moment he was in a happy mood. After fifteen years in the business and some fifty movies—more than half of them silents, very few of them memorable—he was quitting.

Beckoning to him now was the world of New York newspapers and the Broadway stage where he'd begun his writing career as a reporter and drama critic. His wife and three young children he'd left behind in the Mankiewicz house on Tower Road in Beverly Hills. When he'd found a job in New York and had set up an apartment he'd send for them.

At age forty-two, as his friends gladly testified, Mank was a man of sharp intelligence, wide knowledge, and serious intellectual interests, as well as considerable personal charm. He was also one of Hollywood's renowned wits, his quick, biting sallies in conversation often making the rounds next day among insiders. Regrettably, he was also two other things which were not so welcome and which together had blocked his rise in film circles: he was a compulsive gambler, as well as a hopeless alcoholic with almost a daily need for drink. The latter fault often marred what all who knew him agreed was the very real pleasure of his company, especially when he'd get disgustingly sick at a party, or those times when he'd grow belligerent and get himself hurt, or when he'd loudly damn the fate that had condemned him to Hollywood's high-paying but soul-destroying slavery. His early dreams of earning true literary fame as author of acclaimed plays and prize-winning novels had never deserted him.

As so often with talented people who sacrifice ideals for comfort and luxury, Mank was only partly right in feeling that he had great things in him: the superior abilities he demonstrated in person didn't translate readily to the typed or printed page. Never once in his long career as a scriptwriter had he produced true original work of any substance. Aside from occasional flashes of wit and insight, his movie writing was only adequate, professionally dependable but uninspired. Most of the films he'd work on were forgotten before they completed their theater runs as second features. In very few pictures of real worth did he have a hand, never on his own (*Dinner at Eight, Horse Feathers,* and *Million Dollar Legs* were his zenith, on all of which he was one of a team of writers).

Socially, on the other hand, the Mankiewiczes' years in Hollywood had been a decided pleasure, even something of a triumph. Herman and his wife had even been favored with inclusion in the exclusive Hearst circle at San Simeon where during the late twenties and early thirties they were often invited to pay week-long visits. Sara Mankiewicz would tell with astonishment of the marvels in one of their rooms, gold ceilings, fifteenth-century Italian and French furniture, a Flemish stone mantel with terra cotta Madonna and Child from the Middle Ages. "I used to feel that I was walking on air," she'd say of her visits to the enchanted hilltop. Both Hearst and Marion Davies the two often met and spent time with at meals or playing tennis or at the poolside, yet couldn't say they knew either one intimately. Of course like everyone else they'd heard the incessant gossip.

Such delights as hobnobbing with the stars at parties in private estates or on visits to San Simeon, however, though softening the peculiar burdens of Hollywood existence, had never really compensated Herman for everything he felt he'd given up. Only the week before it had all come to a head when he was fired by Louis B. Mayer from his scriptwriting job at MGM (the gambling and the alcohol). That episode had triggered his growing resolve to make a final break with his glamorous, dead-end life. To his wife as he packed his bags he vowed that he was finished with the movies.

By now the speeding car had passed through the town of Victorville and was facing its first open stretch of the Mojave Desert. It was here that the accident happened.

Rain had begun to fall in the afternoon, at first a light spray then a heavy downpour, making the roads dangerously slick. Anxious to reach Vegas before dark, young Phipps sped up and at first was all right, but as he negotiated one long, glistening curve the wheels skidded, the car spun out of control, hit a roadside stanchion, then plunged down a sloping embankment. As it plowed slowly to a stop in the grass it flipped over. Both men were bruised and bloodied, though considering the possibilities for injury in an open car neither was hurt too seriously. Phipps sustained a fractured collarbone. Mank's left leg was badly shattered, broken in three places.

Passing cars alerted the police, who summoned an ambulance to take the injured men back to Los Angeles, and late that evening, after notification to the families, both were checked into Cedars of Lebanon hospital. For some three weeks, wearing a cast from hip to ankle, Mank lay in a hospital bed, then was sent home. No more than two weeks after his arrival back among his family in Beverly Hills the idea of *Citizen Kane* was born. Within another few weeks, after excited discussions with Orson Welles, he began writing the script. By spring of 1940 RKO had given its approval. That July shooting began.

Precisely how it all happened, where the original idea came from, who deserves to be credited with what elements of the world-famed result, are matters that have long occupied film historians, without producing much agreement. But the true story of *Citizen Kane*'s genesis is not so difficult to uncover as has been made out. The necessary clues are all there, if at times a bit twisted and obscure, spread plainly on the record, needing only patient unraveling.

❦

Stretched on his hospital bed, with his encased leg in traction, having little to occupy his thoughts but his family, his mounting debts, and the large mortgage on the Tower Road house, Herman Mankiewicz was a worried man. If he'd managed to reach New York, he knew, he'd have quickly landed a position with any of a half-dozen newspapers and magazines. Now, back in Hollywood and again dependent on the studios, he wasn't at all sure how things would work out. In the days before his departure—for good, as he thought—he hadn't been backward about telling various executives at MGM, and other studios where he did occasional writing, exactly what he thought of them and their trashy, blood-sucking industry. The memory of such outbursts now made him shake his head ruefully.

With three bad fractures in the same leg having to heal, the doctors had warned him that he'd be off his feet for at least a month in the hospital, then afterwards at home would be pretty well restricted for several more months. None of the many friends who came to see him at the hospital, a steady stream, was able to suggest anything practical in the way of employment. The one who finally came to his rescue was Orson Welles, not as a matter of charity but because the Campbell Playhouse needed another scriptwriter.

Back in New York City Welles and Mankiewicz had met once or twice and had liked each other immediately, each impressed by the other's confident style, outspoken wit, wide erudition, and intellectual curiosity. One of their meetings took place at Club 21, the popular nightspot favored by the show crowd. According to John Houseman, who spoke with Welles on his return to the theater from the stimulating encounter, the two had spent the afternoon "vying with each other in wit

Welles in Hollywood with his coauthor on the *Kane* script, Herman Mankiewicz. Aided by Welles and John Houseman, Mank wrote the first version of the screenplay in ten weeks.

and savoir-faire," at last becoming convinced that they were "the two most dashing and gallantly intelligent gentlemen in the Western World. And they were not so far wrong!"

In September 1939 Welles' radio sponsor, the Campbell Soup Company, had finally agreed to let the program originate in California, saving their star the tiring, time-consuming weekly trip back east. The new arrangement created an opening for one additional scriptwriter, and to Welles and his staff Mankiewicz seemed a natural choice. Bedridden as he was, or at least severely hampered, he could easily script adaptations of the popular classics planned for broadcast during the Playhouse's 1939–1940 season (*Ah Wilderness, Beau Geste, Dracula, Count of Monte Christo, Lost Horizon,* etc.). Gratefully Mank accepted, and while still in the hospital began work on his initial assignment, *Rip Van Winkle.* For whatever reason, the script wasn't used, but his next effort was, Agatha Christie's *The Murder of Roger Ackroyd.* It aired on November 12, 1939.

At this same time Welles was having his own difficulties, for his deteriorating situation at RKO had reached the embarrassing stage. The film he'd chosen as his first, *Heart of Darkness,* after months of work and the expenditure of many thousands of dollars, was about to be scrapped. The picture meant to replace it, C. D. Lewis's *The Smiler with a Knife,* had failed to generate any excitement and was also on the way out. Now Welles and his staff were engaged in a furious night-and-day search for ideas, dozens of them being proposed only to be wearily rejected.

Then, early in November, the Huxley novel, *After Many a Summer Dies the Swan,* with its veiled, unflattering portrait of the newspaper and movie tycoon, was published. Partly because it was by the eminent novelist and was set in California, partly because of rumors about its link to Hearst, it promptly became the talk of Hollywood. There was even some brief speculation about its possibly being made into a film, but on that idea the opinion was firmly negative. Not a chance, concluded movie people, not with its focus on so obvious and despicable a Hearst figure, portrayed as woefully ignorant and unscrupulous. No studio would take the risk.

Sales of the book were brisk—ten thousand copies were sold in its first three months, though except in Los Angeles not enough to make it a best-seller. From Hearst, curiously, there came no objection, public or private, nothing of the violent reaction he would shortly exhibit with the Welles film. The reason for his reticence in this case is plain: The fact of the book's being modeled on him and his fairy-tale castle found a voice only in spoken gossip, never in print. In the many reviews written about the Huxley novel (all the leading papers and periodicals carried at least a short notice), there occurred no slightest mention of the Hearst name, no real hint that his career and personality underlay the strange plot. Closest to a revelation in print, perhaps, was a casual comment in the *New Yorker*. The novel's leading character, noted reviewer Clifton Fadiman, "is an Asiatically splendiferous California millionaire. Rumors are rife that Huxley's Mr. Stoyte—three of whose characteristics are penchant for young females, a barbaric artistic taste, and a horror of death—is based on a real personage. This I utterly disbelieve, for no human being . . . could possibly be as loathsome as Huxley's Mr. Stoyte."

Of course Fadiman knew very well who the "real personage" was, but would take no chances with a libel suit by openly stating the name. That same cautious attitude held back reviewers everywhere. It would, of course, have been an awful mistake for Hearst to disturb such welcome silence by making a public objection, and anything he might do in private would quickly become public. Also of course, the limited reach (comparatively) of a serious novel by the intellectual Huxley was quite a different thing from the country-wide impact exerted by a movie. While no doubt seething in anger as he walked the corridors of San Simeon, Hearst could well afford to ignore the Huxley book otherwise.

Familiar with the novel at least since the party held the previous July at the Huxley place in Pacific Palisades, Welles may have read it in manuscript, or he may have waited until the first copies were ready in October. Perhaps he picked it up only after its official appearance in November (that same month it began running as a serial in *Harper's* magazine). In any case, that he did read it, and avidly, is established by the fact that before the year was out he had decided to do what savvy film insiders said couldn't be done, make a movie of the book. Far from being a cause of worry, for Welles the connection with Hearst was the very thing that attracted him.

Never yet asked, not pointedly, is the question of *why* Welles for his first movie deliberately chose to court the enmity of the newspaper tycoon—if asked, certainly it has not been adequately treated. But the answer in any case is glaringly obvious. He did it for no other reason than its stupendous publicity value. If he could pull it off, he knew, he'd create the biggest sensation in Hollywood's nearly forty years of existence. *That* should answer his critics, in the process restoring his slightly tarnished legend as a show business genius. Of course to make such an attempt at all you had to be a *very* young genius, say still in your twenties, when foolhardy things seem not only possible but hugely exciting. You also had to be lucky enough to gain, despite your few years, a position of trust in which you could *do* such unheard-of things. Aside from Welles, was there ever another young Hollywood genius in quite that position?

❂

"A picture based on the Huxley novel?" replied Mankiewicz from his bed to Welles' casual inquiry one day late in November. As he often did now for the pleasure of talking with his friend and to discuss some current Campbell Playhouse script, Welles had dropped by the Tower Road house. The idea of filming the novel Mank had already heard mentioned by several people, though never quite seriously. But Orson looked very serious.

"You wouldn't get away with it," added Mank after a moment's thought. "Hearst would hear about it before you got started, or while you were shooting. He'd come down on you like a ton of bricks. Anyway, RKO would never go for it . . . be fun to try, though, wouldn't it!"

Welles' concept, as he explained it to Mankiewicz, was to anchor the whole story on the Ince affair. Details from real life could be added—the old newspapers were full of interesting bits about Ince's sudden demise—helping to emphasize the threat that Huxley used only as his denouement. Give Huxley's garish treatment of Hearst's life the added appeal of a murder mystery, insisted Welles, build in the same sort of innovative film technique he'd planned for *Heart of Darkness,* and you'd have a smash!

On Welles' next visit to the Tower Road house— the two men, living in Brentwood and Beverly Hills, were almost next-door neighbors—it was Mankiewicz who broached the subject of a Hearst film. Why bother with Huxley, he asked suddenly, why not do something original?

He'd been thinking about his own visits to San Simeon, he went on, remembering his own contacts with Hearst. He'd also been doing some reading, a couple of recent Hearst biographies, each fully documented, neither of them pulling any punches. All the Hearst stuff in the Huxley novel, he said, was a matter of public record, or was available in widespread rumor. Private stuff could come from people like him, people who'd been to San Simeon and were familiar with Hearst and his mistress. Huxley, so far as he could tell, had used both of the biographies as sources, but had been more concerned with getting his own ideas across, and so had left out a lot of really good stuff.

If Welles was interested, suggested Mankiewicz a bit hesitantly, he could rough out a couple of scenes. Already he knew how he'd tell the story. It was a technique he recalled from a movie he'd seen five or six years before, called *The Power and the Glory,* starring Spencer Tracy. In it a wealthy executive dies, and his story is uncovered through a series of flashbacks. Very effective. Just the thing for getting behind the scenes with a man like Hearst.

At this, Welles' mind leapt back to his own early days when he'd been a voice on the popular newsreel *The March of Time.* They could start the picture with a device like that, he said, a segment of *The March of Time* reporting the death of Hearst, or whatever his name might be in the movie, and giving the high points of his life and legend. Then the action would track his true story by searching the memories of the dead man's surviving friends and associates.

"Yeah!" contributed Mankiewicz eagerly, "Hearst is dying and he whispers a message, something mysterious that's overheard by the nurse. Unraveling the tantalizing words takes up the whole picture. Sure it's been used before but if it's done right it always works. Grabs you."

"Good!" offered Welles. "What would he say? Something shadowy, suggestive. . . ."

There was silence as the two men, caught up in the excitement of the developing moment, groped for solid ground. "A few words about himself," ventured Welles. "Something about when he was a boy. Or is that too obvious?"

"Oh it's obvious," replied Mankiewicz. "So is a lot of other stuff that movies get away with over and over."

"Can't have too many words in it," added Welles who was now talking in his old, fast, confident way. "Not if it's to hit home, have real impact. Three or four? Fewer? Maybe only one . . . could you do it with one? It'd have to be something that didn't fit the moment . . . out of place . . . so the audience will wonder. Those two biographies of Hearst you mentioned, I'd like to read them."

"Think you can use me on the picture?" inquired Mankiewicz as he jotted down the names of Lundberg and Carlson/Bates.

"Go ahead. Do a couple of scenes. Do the opening, maybe, the *March of Time* thing. Throw in everything about Hearst you can dig up. We'll trim it later. Use Hearst's name. Later we'll change it."

Catching himself, Welles grew suddenly wary about making a commitment with his often unreliable friend. Mank was an able screenwriter. He was also, to be honest, a lush. Worse, he was currently in one of his troubled periods, call them confused. It had been years since he had done anything worthwhile on film. Radio scripts were different, nowhere near the same thing as writing for a big movie production costing probably a million. The last thing Welles needed now was to get hooked up with a chancy writer, one who might or might not deliver.

"Do the *March of Time* piece," he quietly amended. "Let's see how it comes out. Then we can talk."

Busy with his Campbell Playhouse assignments (*Vanity Fair, Huckleberry Finn)*, Mankiewicz at first couldn't find much time for the Hearst scenes. By late December, however, he had begun, found that the writing went easily, and in early January 1940 he presented Welles with a thirty-page treatment. More than just the *March of Time* segment, it ambitiously depicted the film's whole opening sequence. Reading it, Welles was greatly if unexpectedly impressed. While waiting he had managed to read the two Hearst biographies, and he could see how nicely Mank's opening fit the story:

Closing off a broad road is a huge, iron-grill gateway. At its top the moving camera picks up a large, prominent initial H. Through the opening gates goes the camera, revealing "a literally incredible domain," passes by ruined tennis courts and golf links, and a collection of empty animal cages, then approaches an enormous castle perched on a hilltop, "compounded of several genuine castles of European origin." The castle itself is entered and the camera proceeds into a bedroom where the estate's master lies dying. On the screen, filling it, appears the lower half of the man's face showing a moustache and a pair of enormous lips. The lips part and a hoarse whisper is clearly heard, a single word twice repeated: "Rosebud! . . . Rosebud! . . . Rosebud!" Suddenly, startlingly, breaking into the scene a stentorian, staccato voice announces, "News! On the March!" And an imitation of the familiar newsreel begins to sketch the incredible life of the dead Hearst.

"Rosebud?" asked Welles, sitting by the bed of the propped-up Mankiewicz whose leg was no longer raised in traction but still wore a cast, this one less ponderous. "It's good. Where'd you get it? Does it mean a girl?"

Smiling, Mankiewicz shrugged. "I don't know yet," he admitted. "It'll mean whatever we want it to mean."

"Two syllables," said Welles, "one drawn out, the other more clipped. Seems like two short words yet it's only one. I like it. We'll have to think of a good reason why he says it, why it's on his tongue as he dies. The nurse hears it but he's not talking to her. He's not talking to anyone, just himself. Does he know he's dying?"

"Don't know that yet, either."

"Does the word come to him unexpectedly out of his past," asked Welles. "Or is it something he has often recalled? Is he aware of its meaning for him as he whispers it? Or what?"

"Does it make a difference? I'm not sure it does."

"It might . . . it might . . . of course at the finish of the picture the audience finds out what it means. How do we manage that?"

"Didn't get that far."

"Rosebud. Nice. How did you think of it?"

Mank hesitated. "I'd rather not say. Keeping it a secret will hype the publicity. Sooner or later you'd tell someone else and it'd get out. But if you insist—"

"I insist."

"I happened to hear it years ago at San Simeon."

"You mean it's actually connected with Hearst?"

"So I'm told. Maybe it's true, maybe not. Seems when Hearst was younger he used it to refer to a certain part of his mistress's anatomy."

"A pet name for Marion? What part?"

Mank laughed. "The polite word I think is pudenda."

Welles joined the laugh. "How'd you pick up information like that? Who told you? Not Marion herself!"

"No," said Mank, smiling. "Not Marion. One of her friends."

"Well, *who*!"

"Maybe I shouldn't—"

"Oh come on! It makes a difference, a big difference, if there's some reality to the story, if there's an actual source. . . ."

"Louise Brooks. You know, the old silent film actress. She's one of Marion's best pals. Always visiting her at San Simeon. I knew her from the old days."

"Must have been *some* conversation! Just the two of you?"

"Yeah. I forget just how it came up. We'd both had a couple. She was going on about Hearst, how he was so proper in public while in private he—"

"Where'd Brooks get it?"

"From Marion of course."

"She said so? Said she heard it straight from Marion?"

"Yeah."

"Did it seem right to you? I mean would Marion talk so openly about such intimate—"

"Yeah, she would," replied Mank, shaking his head. "With her close women friends, yeah she would. Louise especially. Marion's friends were important to her, shut off the way she was in the gilded cage. . . ."

Again Welles laughed. "Serve the old goat right if we did use it in the picture. *Rosebud,* he whispers as he dies! That'd get his full attention!"

"What about that, Orson? I mean getting Hearst's attention. What happens if you do a picture exposing him as brutally as Huxley does? He's a dangerous man to cross. A picture is seen by millions. That's a whole lot different from a book. You know he won't let you get away with—"

Welles brushed the question aside. "We'll worry about that later," he said abruptly. "Hearst isn't that big."

The writing contract Welles offered his friend in mid-January was happily accepted, with little discussion. It paid Mankiewicz a thousand dollars a week (the Campbell contract paid him two hundred a week), for as long as the writing took, estimated at about three months. If the finished script was found satisfactory and was completed on time a bonus of five thousand would be added.

In the matter of credit almost the same arrangement was made as for the Campbell agreement. Welles' own contract with RKO called for him to produce, direct, star in, and write his own movies, the fourfold function to be part of the "boy genius" publicity campaign. This did not preclude Welles getting help with the writing, but in any case authorship was to be attributed to him alone. This Mankiewicz understood perfectly, and it was an arrangement that bothered no one. All were aware that an initial script by Mankiewicz, or by anyone else, would be carefully worked over by Welles, who as usual would make wholesale changes. Nobody expected the first version of a film script to be ready for shooting.

⊕

The writing took only ten weeks. Nearly four hundred manuscript pages of productive writing had been crammed into seventy-two smooth, steady days. All of them were spent, not at Mank's Beverly Hills home but at a small resort cottage in the town of Victorville. That was the same little town on the edge of the Mojave Desert Mankeiwicz had passed through just prior to his accident. With him at Victorville were John Houseman, a nurse, and a secretary. Sensibly, Welles had decided that there was only one way to be sure that work on the script would not be interrupted by the writer going off on a drinking binge or growing bored and defeated and quitting, or working at too leisurely a pace. He needed to be physically isolated, far from temptation or the possibility of intrusion. He also needed to have beside him a steadying hand, someone he could talk with about the developing story and who could do preliminary editing on each day's completed pages, someone Mankiewicz knew and liked. That meant John Houseman, and when Welles asked him to come back from New York and take the assignment he agreed without a murmur. By then he had forgiven Welles for what he lightly referred to as "the night of the flaming sternos."

Years later Houseman remembered those strangely placid yet crucial weeks at Victorville. Following a frank talk with the Mankiewiczes at the Tower Road

The Victorville cottage, east of Hollywood, in which Mankiewicz (center) and John Houseman (right) lived while writing the *Kane* script. Welles (left) was an occasional visitor.

The Hollywood studios of RKO at Gower and Melrose Streets. Most of *Citizen Kane* was shot here

house, he phoned Welles his acceptance of the job, then promptly signed a contract with Mercury Productions. Two days later—loaded down with research materials including the Huxley novel and the two recent Hearst biographies, those by Lundberg and Carlson and Bates, as well as everything else available on Hearst in print, and carrying a thick sheaf of suggestions by Welles—the adventure began. Agreed between the two was the junking of the Ince affair as the story's mainspring. What would replace it was left pretty much to Mankiewicz to decide:

> We set out for the San Bernardino mountains in a small caravan that consisted of a studio limousine containing Mankiewicz prone and protesting in the back seat, with a trained nurse and two pairs of crutches in the front, and a convertible driven by myself, containing a secretary, a typewriter, three cases of stationery, and research material. That night the limousine departed and the next day we went to work. . . .
>
> Our life was austere but comfortable . . . with no distractions for a hundred miles around. . . . Mank and I shared a bungalow with two bedrooms and a living room which we used as a study. . . . The mental and emotional energy which Mank had squandered for years in self-generated conflicts and neurotic disorders was now concentrated on the single task of creating our script. After so many fallow years his fertility was amazing.

Reading and writing half the night, Mankiewicz slept late in the mornings. Houseman rose early, ate breakfast in the main house, went riding for an hour, then edited the pages Mank had dictated the night before, typed up by the secretary at dawn. About nine-thirty Mank received his breakfast in bed and an hour later—"having made an enormous production of shaving and dressing himself on one leg"—was again ready for work. First he'd go over the previous day's material, arguing with Houseman about even small changes, and noting how the new scenes fitted into the overall structure, and how they influenced upcoming scenes:

> We were not entirely incommunicado. Sarah drove up every other week to satisfy herself that all was well, and seemed astounded to discover that it was. Orson telephoned at odd hours to inquire after our progress, then on the appointed day at the end of six weeks he arrived in a limousine . . . read a hundred pages of script, listened to our outline of the rest, dined with us at The Green Spot, thanked us and returned to Los Angeles. . . .
>
> Finally after ten weeks we were done. . . . The script was more than four hundred pages long—overrich, repetitious, loaded with irrelevant, fascinating detail and private jokes, of which we loved every one.

Back in Los Angeles the two did some drastic last-minute editing, and late in April 1940 the finished product, reduced to less than three hundred pages, a more reasonable length, and titled simply *American,* was handed to Welles. He found it very good, acceptable as a start but inevitably needing a great deal of refinement, a judgment with which both Mank and Houseman readily agreed.

Aside from faulty logic and simple errors of continuity, the script displayed other more troubling defects, for instance a decided lack of subtlety in the characters. They were all—but especially that of Kane/Hearst—far too rigid, without shading, and as a result less compelling than required for dramatic impact. A defect or weakness even more obvious was the way the separate incidents of Hearst's career, the mundane as well as the more notorious, had been larded into the story one after the other with little attempt to evoke a pattern or meaning. They had, it appeared, been transferred almost bodily from the printed sources, with the result that, taken together, they loudly proclaimed the identity of the film's real-life model. The glaring link with Hearst amounting nearly to an indictment couldn't be missed by anyone who read the papers, which became a fact that *did,* as even Welles confessed, cause serious legal problems. If left unchanged the existing script would certainly bring from RKO a swift rejection.

Through May and into June, alone or with Mank's help, Welles worked over the script, cutting, trimming, dropping scenes and adding new ones, and extensively rewriting the dialogue. In the process he managed to mute much of the Hearst-related material while adding depth to the character, also mixing in some extraneous matter so that any too-blatant Hearst link could be credibly denied. When he finished his doctoring, the script had been reduced by almost another hundred pages and vastly improved. The critic who has made the most searching study of the various surviving versions found that Welles' skillful rewriting created or strengthened a certain aspect of the story: "the narrative brilliance—the visual and verbal wit, the stylistic fluidity, and such stunningly original strokes as the newspaper montage and the breakfast table sequence. He also transformed Kane from a cardboard fictionalization of Hearst into a figure of mystery and epic magnificence."

In submitting the final script to George Schaeffer and the studio lawyers, Welles understandably held his breath. Was the link with Hearst still too obvious, too heavy-handed? Would the always cautious legal staff declare it still too risky? If they did, who would Schaeffer listen to, his lawyers or his brilliant star?

Early in June came the decision. Surprisingly, there had been no strong objection by the legal department. As a result, on Schaeffer's personal authority, overcoming some grumbling by a few minor executives, the script was approved. The legitimate question as to why RKO so blithely took on so formidable a target, why it plunged headlong into what it must have suspected might prove a maelstrom, because of the absence of evidence must remain unclarified. If credit for commendable daring goes to anyone in particular at the studio, it must be the man in charge, the man who had the last word, George Schaeffer. Later, Welles himself called Schaeffer "a hero."

The budget for the picture, at first reckoned by studio estimators at over a million dollars, was finally pared down to just over $800,000. The figure was still high but, given the number of sets needed (an unprecedented eighty-one) and the list of special effects planned (contained in nearly half the final footage), not exorbitant.

With that, Schaeffer made his most direct and telling contribution to the film itself. It was he who, refining an early attempt at a title by Welles *(John Citizen, USA),* came up with the perfect one: *Citizen Kane.*

5

On the Set

"We're only making tests. I haven't started shooting yet," lied Orson Welles to Schaeffer on an RKO soundstage two weeks after shooting on *Kane* had begun in earnest.

Secrecy, as tight as possible, and a total grasp of production were now Welles' main concerns. The different sets, whether at the big lot on Gower Street or at other RKO locations in the city, were to be strictly controlled. No visitors would be permitted except if invited by Welles, and only by Welles. Even the studio's own executives were barred, the willing Schaeffer included. Cast and crew had standing orders, if an intruder did slip by the guards, to halt work and start an impromptu softball game, for which a ball and bat were kept handy, and several times during the filming were used.

For as long as he could manage it while shooting, Welles wanted to keep from press and public any word of his bold film, and particularly from the man most concerned, Hearst himself. The tycoon would hear of it when and how Welles was ready for him to hear of it, and not, he hoped, till then. Even with all the secrecy, however, with so many people involved, he feared that it might not be long before the truth seeped out. The mere fact of RKO closing a set in itself became news. "Mr. Welles is conducting secret film tests of himself," reported the *New York Times* in August, "in a secret role in a secret picture."

The filming schedule approved by the studio allowed for a three-month shoot, the picture to be in the can by the end of October. Casting and rehearsals, continuity sketches and model making for set design, the building of the sets themselves, and a start on the music, all had gone smoothly and were well advanced. To everyone's great relief—and for some not a little surprise—the neophyte director quickly demonstrated a master's touch, shaping a medium new to him as if he'd been born to it. His rapport with his actors was instant and knowing. His ability when needed to lift them above themselves in performance was both uncanny and unfailing, and much appreciated.

In the end he directed nearly six hundred separate scenes, in many of which he himself appeared. In the Hollywood of the time a star directing his own performance was a very rare thing, almost never done. Welles approached it by having his stand-in play the scene while he directed, then repeating it for the camera with himself in place.

His stunningly imaginative use of the camera— guided by the industry's most technically innovative and daring cinematographer, Gregg Toland—his sure manipulation of lighting, sound, and physical space, repeatedly brought to the mind of watchers the old label of genius. When in make-up and costume he also took his place on the set as the picture's star, displaying a startling virtuosity as an actor—he ages some fifty years in the part—the impression of him as a show business marvel unmatched in Hollywood history was complete.

Photographer Toland in particular was mightily impressed by his young and energetic colleague, later saying that the time he spent on *Kane* "was indeed the most exciting professional adventure of my career." By then Toland, in his seventeen years behind the camera, had filmed almost forty movies, had experienced every kind and sort of director, encountered virtually every possible camera situation and problem. Of the neophyte Welles—less than a year after completion of *Kane,* when the experience was still fresh in his mind— he had this to say:

> He proved one of the most cooperative artists with whom it has been my privilege to work. He let down all bars on originality of photographic effects and angles. . . . He is unique in his zeal to get exactly what

he wants. We spent four days perfecting one very difficult shot. It was a complex mixture of art and mechanics. A table and chair on rollers were to behave
with clock-like precision as a three-ton camera boom
moved over them. . . . When the props behaved on
schedule, a child actor would blow up his line. When
those two items were co-ordinated, the operation of
the camera crane by nine men would be out of synch.
To bring all this action, dialogue, and mechanics into
perfect time was the problem. . . .

[Another time] we made fifteen takes of a scene
without obtaining one that was perfect. When the
dialogue was right, the mechanics were off. Or it was
the other way around. I suggested that we match the
perfect sound track of one take with the flawless pho-
tographic mechanics of another. Welles agreed. The
experiment was a success.

Welles was emphatic, recalled Toland, that the standard Hollywood approach to cinematography, all the
old tried-and-true techniques, "should go hang if need
be." Long before shooting began, specific camera usage
was under intense discussion, precise plans being laid.
That in itself, said Toland, was unusual in Hollywood,
"where most cinematographers learn of their next assignments only a few days before the shooting starts.
Altogether I was on the job for a half-year," including
preparation, shooting, and follow-up.

Though it was Welles' first effort at movie-making,
ends Toland in high admiration, "he came to the job

Mr. Mars Goes to Hollywood

...Orson Welles, whose man-from Mars broadcast scared radio listeners a while-back, now is a movie director—at $150,000 for making, and acting in,

Citizen Kane. He's 25 and plays the role 'of a 76-year-old man.·The cup?·.Tea, his favorite beverage.
— Photos by Wide World

The New York newspaper *PM* on August 2, 1940, gave a full page to this photo of Orson Welles in Hollywood directing a scene from *Citizen Kane*. "Mr. Mars" refers to his radio broadcast of 1938.

with a rare vision and understanding of camera purpose and direction."

Most wonderful of all, the shooting sped along on
schedule and without interruption, whether from accident, artistic temperament, or unexpected hitches in
the storyline needing correction. Even a broken ankle,
suffered by Welles when he tripped while shooting a
scene which had him hurrying down a twisting flight
of stairs, didn't interfere for more than a day. Taken to a
hospital he had the ankle set and put in a cast. Next
morning he showed up on the set in a wheelchair, the
affected leg held out straight, and shooting of an alter-
nate scene began.

The working days were long, though, often for
many of the cast beginning at five or six in the morning and lasting to late evening. More than once, as
Welles would recall, shooting "went on for twenty-four
hours around the clock, with nobody going to bed," in
order to complete a sequence that threatened to hold
up production.

Yet he was not without shortcomings, especially of
the sort caused by inexperience. For example, he was
notorious for the number of takes he might call for on
a scene before shouting, "Cut and print!" Regularly it
ran into the dozens, sometimes reaching an incredible
hundred or more. "One day on a scene," recalled an
actor involved in the incident, "he shot more than
three thousand meters of film! But he printed *nothing*
from that day's work! Then the next day he got the shot

in two takes." The same actor remembered how one brief scene involving a single player uttering only a dozen words was rehearsed for an entire morning, at least three hours. Then it was run through more than twenty takes before Welles was satisfied.

Such excesses, of course, were not always what has been claimed, a commendable drive for perfection. They were often a result of the director not knowing what he wanted or how to get it until he saw it, the unfailing sign of a beginner. As Welles worked, he learned, but was able by his manner to cloak the fact, making it all seem wonderfully painstaking.

A second example of Welles' inexperience also concerns excess, in this case a deliberate effort to break through inhibitions, and inevitably overdoing it. In reply to an interviewer's question some years afterward Welles agreed that in *Kane,* "there are more conscious shots—for the sake of shots—than in anything I've done since. . . . There's a kind of unjustified visual strain at times which came from the exuberance of discovering the medium, and once you get used to it and learn how to swim you don't have to flex so many muscles." While making the film, of course, he voiced no such thought.

Only a single description of Welles at work on the set reached print at the time, and that was toward the end of shooting when he began to think about publicity. By invitation a reporter from the *San Francisco Chronicle* came to the Gower Street lot one day about mid-October, not to watch as the cameras rolled but for a rehearsal. Whether what he saw and recorded was a legitimate day's work for Welles and the cast, or was a performance for the reporter's benefit, or was a little of both, isn't easy to decide:

> On the day we were there the rehearsal went like this: Having picked up the cover of a property garbage pail, Welles held it over his chest like a shield and said, "Lay on McDuff, and damned be he who first cries hold enough!"
>
> Then, while his actors responded to this unorthodox rehearsal call and shambled into place, the boy continued with a few more of the words Shakespeare wrote. One actor corrected him and another actor picked up where he left off and the whole thing turned out to be very sprightly, not at all like the boss blowing the work whistle and telling his lugs to demonstrate what they were getting paid for.
>
> Well, that proved one reason why Welles had become a big-shot boss at the age of 26, and another one turned up a few minutes later when an actor old enough to have Welles as one of his pups started to get on the boss's nerves. The boss expressed his irritation in classic mode, but expressed it nevertheless. "Soandso," he said, and flung both fists on high, "Don't!" He seemed to realize that was harsh and added, "Don't, don't . . . don't let your animal spirits get the better of you!" He was fighting for control of himself. His fists remained on high and he didn't appear able to think of a way to get them down. "Your animal spirits," he cried, his fists trembling violently, "are very . . . very . . . very high, you know."

There was considerable tension over the company for a time after that, in fact a little sulking, and Welles chose a subtle way out of it—a way that would dissipate the sullenness without impairing the position of the boss. The same actor had a line to say, "All right, I'll give you ten minutes, and I'll call the cops." Welles professed himself unsatisfied with the way the line was being read. Finally he told the actor, "Just give it to me in your own words." The actor was embarrassed.

"Just give me the sense of that line in your own words, what you yourself would say in that situation," pressed Welles. The actor looked unblinkingly at Welles for a moment and then said, "Well, I would say, I would put it . . . I mean . . . I'd say it, 'Looka here, you got ten minutes and then I'll break your neck.'"

He was looking directly into Welles' eyes when he said it and Welles laughed uproariously. "I bet you would break my neck," roared Welles and flung his arms around the actor and hugged him and told him that he was marvelous and priceless. After that the whole company went back to loving the boss to death, and to thinking he was easily the greatest guy the Lord had ever set on earth.

So you see there is a little more to Welles than making noise, and a little more to Welles than the fact that he has made more people pay attention to and get excited about serious art than anybody his age or even older now on earth—and a little more to him than the fact that he is colorful and comical and precocious and an actor, writer, producer, director of stage screen and radio.

It is plain that on the set Welles was not always an even-tempered or calming presence. He was "marvelously exciting, stimulating, maddening, frustrating," was the way one colleague put it. "He could one moment be guilty of a piece of behavior so outrageous as to make you want to tell him to go to hell and walk off the set. Before you could do it he would come up with some idea so brilliant it would literally have your mouth gaping open."

From time to time the sets did have other outside visitors, carefully chosen and shepherded by Welles who selected days on which the scene being shot was unrevealing. The two leading gossip columnists, Hedda Hopper and Louella Parsons, were among the few given such access. For good reason his reception of Parsons in September was more formal than that accorded her rival about a week later. A longtime Hearst employee, Parsons' avidly read column ran regularly in all Hearst papers, and to Welles since his arrival in Hollywood she had devoted a good deal of space. "He photographs like a million dollars," she gushed in one column, predicting that the girls of America would soon "sigh over young Welles."

On the set at RKO Welles received her in his own dressing room and had her served with a five-course luncheon, all the while chatting freely about his movie. In her column next day, quoting Welles, she gave the first public description of the picture: "It deals with a dead man. You know that when a man dies there is often a great difference of opinion about his character. In the picture I have everyone voice his opinion, and no two descriptions are alike." The Hearst connection wasn't even hinted.

To Hopper during her visit to the set, because she had also mentioned him frequently and favorably in her column, Welles made a promise to have her, and not her chief rival Louella, at the picture's first press showing. Probably be in January, he said. Smilingly she accepted and said she'd hold him to it.

Even before the picture was finished Welles pulled a sort of preliminary publicity stunt involving some agile maneuvering behind the scenes. Its main object apparently was to float the name of Hearst in connection with the picture—Welles of course standing ready to pronounce an indignant denial of any such link. No outright record remains of the rather Byzantine little scheme, only a few stray facts, their true meaning missed until now. Mankiewicz and Welles' own estranged wife, Virginia, who had also moved to Hollywood, would be his instruments.

Somehow, completely unexpectedly, the now fancy-free Virginia had met and become involved with a man, also a screenwriter, who was a nephew of Marion Davies, the son of her sister Reine. No one knows just when or exactly how the meeting of the two occurred, but thoughts of marriage were soon in the air (the two did marry, and rather quickly, in a ceremony that took place at San Simeon in February 1941). The man's name was Charles Lederer, brother of the actor Francis Lederer, and he was in fact a favorite with his aunt, spending much time visiting her with his mother at San Simeon. Further complicating the situation, Herman Mankiewicz himself was a good friend of Lederer and often ran into him in Los Angeles.

Word-of-mouth rumor in Hollywood—*not* yet in the papers—had already breathed the name of Hearst in connection with the movie: with so many people involved it was impossible to prevent *some* talk. Then approaching mid-September, at Welles' direction Mankiewicz gave a copy of the *Kane* script to Lederer, who at Virginia's urging had asked to see it. In his ex-wife's mind, probably during one of his visits to see his daughter who was then living with her mother in Hollywood, Welles had managed to plant a suspicion about the movie, particularly as to its treatment of Marion.

Only it wasn't a copy of the *Kane* script, not a true copy of the veritable shooting script. It was a shorter preliminary treatment of the story in which the portraits of Hearst and Marion were subordinated and softened, gentled down to the point of being innocuous, even in a way romanticized. What happened next can only be guessed at, the guessing considerably enlivened by a stray item that appeared in mid-September in the pages of *Newsweek*. In a column of miscellaneous chit-chat, this suddenly occurs: "The script of Orson Welles' first movie, 'Citizen Kane,' was sent to William Randolph Hearst for perusal after columnists had hinted that it dealt with his life. Hearst approved it without comment."

Welles' response to that and similar statements over the ensuing weeks was nicely calculated. *Citizen Kane* isn't about Hearst at all, he would insist: "It is a portrait of a fictional newspaper tycoon, and I have never said or implied that it is anything else. . . . I have met some publishers, but I know none of them well enough to make them possible as models."

For the first time in print the name of Hearst had appeared alongside that of the movie. It would be far from the last.

❀

In tracing Hearst's personal role in the battle over *Citizen Kane,* what is said of him in the following pages rests on direct documentary evidence, and on inescapable inference from those same documents, their plain implications. It is with eminently good and convincing reason that his marauding hand is discovered behind every move made against *Kane* by others on his behalf. Perhaps not surprisingly, some of his more recent biographers have tried to make it seem otherwise. Hearst's underlings, they can actually be heard insisting or at least suggesting, in much of what was perpetrated acted without his knowledge.

On the contrary, everything—*no* exceptions—that was done during four months at the start of 1941 to derail and kill the movie *Citizen Kane* was done on

Hearst's explicit orders and direction. Always those orders were delivered in person or by phone, never in writing, most emanating from that sumptuous San Simeon
office. It was a method of operating which his volumi-
nous collected papers, now available for study in various
California archives, abundantly prove to have been followed throughout his life. His extreme care to leave behind no clearly incriminating written evidence of his
long and outrageous career of freebootery is palpable.

It wasn't a matter of covering his tracks. As one of
the worlds' wiliest scoundrels and wealthiest men he
left very few tracks.

6

Stranded

"Chief, it's me," said Hedda Hopper into the telephone, calling Hearst by the nickname he openly preferred and which was duly used even by his closest associates. "I've just come from an advance screening of the Orson Welles picture."

She paused, thinking how best to say it, how to soften the blow. Then she blurted, "Chief, it's about you—all about you! It's really awful! They've made a . . . *joke* . . . out of Marion! It's not fair!"

For several seconds she listened as Hearst talked. Then, growing calmer, she answered his questions one by one.

"There's no doubt, Chief, none. You can't miss it. I don't care what they showed you before. The movie is about you, your life, your private life, your whole career, and it's *ugly*! It's about Marion, too. They've made her an opera singer, not an actress. But she doesn't have any *voice,* not really. *You* make her a star, I mean Kane does, *you* force her on the public by spending millions on her singing career and praising her to the skies in your newspapers. . . . Yes, they do show her drinking . . . and they show her working on those big jigsaw puzzles just the way Marion does. . . ."

She paused again, listening. "No, she's nothing like Marion is really. No smiles, no sense of fun. Just a shallow, gloomy girl, always complaining in the most grating, screechy voice. At least her name's different. She's called Susan something. . . . What? Ince? No, there's nothing about Ince or how he died. It's not based on the Huxley book, so far as I can tell. The plot's different and it doesn't have the same sort of characters. But I think they did use some of Huxley's scenes. There's one where Huxley has Stoyte breaking up a room in a fit of anger, smashing furniture and pictures and everything. They kept that. Kane goes wild and destroys Susan's bedroom with his bare hands—"

Again she paused. "Why he does it? Because Susan gets fed up and finally leaves him . . . yes, that part is different. In the picture she's your wife not your . . . uh, that is, I mean your first wife dies, I mean Kane's first wife, and you marry this Susan, a little anemic, whining creature of no talent, not really, and when she walks out he goes berserk and . . . but Chief, there's one thing I didn't get. Does the word *Rosebud* mean anything to you? . . . Chief? Did you hear me? *Rosebud.* Does it mean anything."

Abruptly, without a word, Hearst had hung up.

That conversation, or something very much like it, according to Hedda Hopper herself took place on the morning of January 4, 1941. Several days passed, then on the morning of the eighth the phone in Welles' RKO office rang. It was Louella Parsons. Barely taking time to say hello, in a cool tone very unlike her usual warm manner towards him, she requested an immediate private showing of his film. For herself, she said, and one or two others. The reason she gave for the peremptory request was personal: her rival, her principal competitor in the business of gathering Hollywood news, had been favored with a screening. She demanded no less. In her column she had been equally good to the wonder boy and was certainly entitled to equal treatment by him.

Welles, expecting the call, knowing well who had instigated it, perfectly aware that the "one or two others" would be Hearst lawyers, apologized for his oversight. If Louella would come right over he'd be happy to run the picture for her and her guests, or whenever it was convenient.

She'd be there first thing in the morning, she answered.

Of all those who rallied to Hearst's command, becoming loyal henchmen, and hatchet-men, in his all-out war against *Kane,* Welles, and RKO, Louella Parsons was the only one with a personal, in fact a true emotional tie to the subject. Some seventeen years before, just as she was beginning to gain a name as a

Hearst in party costume poses with Hedda Hopper, Hollywood gossip columnist.

Louella Parsons writes about Marion Davies. Both Hopper and Parsons had a hand in Hearst's vendetta against *Citizen Kane* and Orson Welles.

movie columnist, she had accepted Hearst's offer to switch over from the *New York Telegraph* at twice the salary ($250 weekly, handsome pay at the time for an obscure journalist). Relentlessly spotlighted in the entire Hearst chain, she soon gathered a huge readership, growing into the country's most influential purveyor of movieland gossip—and not incidentally doing her part to boost the career of Marion Davies, no small part of the reason Hearst signed her to start with.

What Parsons really thought of Davies' acting talents isn't known. With Davies herself, however, she did form a real and lasting friendship. At their first meeting, about 1923 as she recalled, with Davies already the star of Hearst's Cosmopolitan Productions, she "expected to find a haughty star . . . instead I found a golden-haired girl, little more than a child, who was dressed in a simple blue suit that a schoolgirl might have worn, and who spoke with a confused and delightful little stammer. It was impossible for anyone to meet Marion Davies and not like her." (How much that description fits Huxley's picture of Marion Davies' "child-like innocence"!)

Hearst, too, she liked, going so far as to think him a truly great man and saying so, a man whose evil reputation, she felt sure, had resulted from his always being misunderstood. "Where are there words," she wails in her autobiography, "to express the greatness and understanding of this man who is so often vilified by people who do not know him?" The comment accompanies her recital of the fact that once when she suffered through a lengthy illness and was unable to work, Hearst kept her on full salary: "Such loyalty, such kindness seemed more than I could bear." As he did so often, Hearst had used a situation, Louella's illness, to buy himself another faithful advocate.

Many of the happiest days of her life, Parsons naively admits, were spent in the extravagant confines of San Simeon, and of her untold hours of pleasure there "the gayest and best occasions" were always "the Chief's" birthday, April 29. At a festive banquet held on that day, she recalled, those who really knew the man readily and happily gave him "the love and good wishes that are in our hearts for him every day." Her autobiography, in which she offers these remarks, was published in 1943, when Hearst was still very much alive, and still playing the fabulous host to his friends.

At the RKO lot on the morning of January 9, 1941, Welles greeted a stony-faced Louella. Flanking her on either side like an armed escort were two men whom she introduced as Oscar Lawler and Laurence Mitchell. The fact that they were high-powered Los Angeles attorneys serving on Hearst's legal staff she didn't bother to mention. When all were seated in the narrow projection room the lights were dimmed and the two-hour movie started. Making himself available for the inevitable questions and discussion afterward, Welles took a seat by himself at the room's rear.

He was not quite prepared, when the film had been running about an hour and a half and had reached the dramatic scene in which an enraged Kane smashes up the departed Susan's bedroom, to see Parsons' plump, shadowy figure suddenly stand up, gather her coat from the seat behind her, walk swiftly up the aisle and out the door, letting it slam closed.

Still in their seats, her two companions turned to look after her, then swung their attention back to the film. At its end they too rose and departed, less precipitously but also without a word.

For two days there was silence. Then on the morning of January 11 in the *New York Times* appeared this story:

HEARST OBJECTS TO WELLES FILM
Mention of RKO in His Press Barred as the
Withdrawal of "Citizen Kane" is Demanded

STUDIO HEAD UNMOVED
Schaeffer Says "No Serious Consideration" Is Given—
Actor Denies Biography Intent

Hollywood, Calif., Jan 10—Suppression of the motion-picture "Citizen Kane," Orson Welles' first film venture, has been demanded of RKO-Radio Pictures, Inc., by representatives of William Randolph Hearst the publisher.

It was learned here tonight, coincident with the

request that the $800,000 picture be shelved, that or-
ders have been issued to the heads of all Hearst newspapers barring mention of RKO or its products. The
situation is also said to have created a sharp division
in the RKO forces.

While both the studio and Mr. Hearst's representatives have declined comment, it was learned that
Louella O. Parsons, motion picture editor of International News Services; Oscar Lawler and A. Laurence Mitchell, two Los Angeles attorneys for the
publisher, viewed "Citizen Kane" yesterday and that
Miss Parsons telephoned George Schaeffer, president
of RKO in New York, demanding that the picture be
withdrawn.

The film, which Mr. Welles wrote, directed, produced and in which he appears in the title role, deals
with the life of a fabulously wealthy man who inher-
its a newspaper and builds a publishing empire. . . .
Insistent that "Citizen Kane" is in no wise biographical, Mr. Welles said: "It is not based upon the life of
Mr. Hearst or anyone else. On the other hand, had
Mr. Hearst and similar financial barons not lived
during the period we discuss, "Citizen Kane" could
not have been made."

He declared that Mr. Schaeffer has assured him
that the studio would not abandon the film. It is
understood, however, that before any decision is
made Floyd Odlum of the Atlas Corporation and
David Sarnoff of RCA, both heavily interested in
RKO stock, will be consulted.

Added to the story is a separate trailer paragraph:
"George Schaeffer, president of RKO-Radio Pictures,

said here last night that his company has given 'no serious consideration' to the thought of withholding 'Citizen Kane' from release."

Parsons' phone call to George Schaeffer—probably
on the morning of the tenth after she'd made her report
in person to Hearst on the ninth—did much more
than demand that "the picture be withdrawn," as the
Times phrased it. Wasting no breath on preliminaries,
strictly following Hearst's angry directions, she issued
specific threats. If release of the offending movie was
not promptly and publicly canceled, and the negative
and all prints locked away pending further discussion,
Hollywood itself, the industry as a whole, would come
under attack.

First to suffer would be the studio heads, men
whose personal lives perhaps couldn't stand too much
scrutiny. "Mr. Hearst says if you boys want private
lives," blithely warned the columnist, "then we'll give
you private lives." A staff of crack Hearst investigative
reporters, she added, was even then getting its instruc-
tions, and a blizzard of revealing, tell-all articles in the
Hearst papers about Tinsel-town and the men who ran
it could be expected. Among the writers enlisted was
the well-known Adela Rogers St. Johns, whose assignment was Orson Welles himself, with the emphasis not
on his film career, but on his much-rumored after-
hours activities among Hollywood's leading ladies.

Hanging up on the considerably shaken RKO president, Parsons began making other calls, speaking

frankly to such other influential studio heads as Joseph
Schenck, Darryl Zanuck, and David Selznick. There
was big trouble coming for all, she openly threatened,
unless Schaeffer and RKO were stopped and *Citizen
Kane* killed, the film master and prints all destroyed.
They could take her word for it, she added, because she
was speaking for the aggrieved Hearst himself, which
they could if they wished verify by a confidential word
to attorneys Lawler and Mitchell at their Los Angeles
office.

The charge that Hearst, through Parsons, actually
made such threats against his fellow Hollywood moguls has sometimes been doubted. If it happened at all,
say the doubters, it was the rabid, fumbling Parsons
alone who dreamed up and delivered those clumsy
threats, never telling her boss. No hard evidence, they
insist, supports the accusation. But such evidence does
exist, contemporary with the incident. Within weeks
of Parsons' phone calls to the executives a story appeared in the New York paper *PM* revealing all. It was
written by Ben Hecht, Hollywood insider and close
friend of Herman Mankiewicz. Himself a former
screenwriter, then a staffer on *PM,* in his flip style
Hecht wrote frankly, unlike most who took on Hearst,
boldly naming names:

> Nobody has taken the trouble to get the facts straight
> about the mysterious suppression of Orson Welles
> movie *Citizen Kane.* . . . Concerning the suppression
> of the Welles' picture there has been infinitely less

written than on the heady topic of whose hand Franchot Tone is holding this week. . . . I can assure you it
was not done by Mr. Hearst hollering at Mr. Schaeffer under whose aegis the movie was made. Nor was
it done by Mr. Hearst threatening Mr. Schaeffer with
law suits plus his journalistic wrath. . . .

Mr. Schaeffer stood up very calmly to all of Mr.
Hearst's Fie Fo Fums. This Schaeffer of RKO is as
tough a gentleman to frighten as you will find
under any initialed enterprise, including that of the
RAF. . . .

Mr. Hearst's next move was to seek out a softer
and sappier target. This he found in the person of
Louis B. Mayer, the Grand Poo Bah of Hollywood.
He is producing head of Metro-Goldwyn–Mayer,
and is not only the highest salaried genius on earth
but the oracle to which Hollywood bends its ever
deferential ear.

Mr. Hearst told Mr. Mayer that if the picture was
released, he, Mr. H., had a medium for offering the
country biographical studies of great men every bit as
powerful as the screen. This is almost a verbatim
quote. . . . [Mayer] appealed to the Board of Directors and to the bankers who are behind the financing
of RKO and similar moviemaking organizations. He
told them that Mr. Hearst by attacking something
called Hollywood would alienate the public from the
movies and everybody would lose money. This is not
what Mr. Hearst said. What Mr. Hearst said, with
Talleyrand cunning, was that he would expose
Hollywood's "great men," just as he was being ex-
posed, allegedly, in *Citizen Kane*—and do it in his
newspapers.

Mr. Mayer, knight of the cinema world, won the day for Mr. Hearst. W. R. won't write anything wrong about Mr. Mayer or about any of the other sachems of Hollywood. All this must come as a surprise to the many admirers of Mr. Mayer, and of his co-moguls. For who would have thought that these rajahs had anything to conceal or were afraid of a little literature in the Hearst press?

The ban on mention of RKO and its picture in the Hearst press also went into immediate effect. Reviews and advertisements, for instance, of RKO's newest film, then in national release, *Kitty Foyle,* starring Ginger Rogers, had just started to run, some papers also carrying a serial reprint of the novel it was based on. Without explanation all this was summarily dropped. Except in a few unexplained instances (the *New York Mirror,* for one) during more than a year no RKO-related material would appear in a Hearst paper.

Also reporting on what was shaping up as an ugly fight was the *New York Herald-Tribune,* though it did so in a slightly amused tone, and while actually managing to avoid all use of Hearst's name. It was taking no chances with the aroused tycoon:

A TEMPEST IN HOLLYWOOD'S TEAPOT

By Thornton Delehanty

Hollywood—Orson Welles' faculty for turning on the hot water and then stepping into it up to his neck is perhaps the brightest and most exercised facet of his versatile talent. This last week Hollywood has been set on its ear over the controversy between the youthful Welles and a certain publisher over what the latter maintains is a trespass on himself.

This is said to occur in Welles' portrait of a Czaristic publisher in "Citizen Kane," his forthcoming picture which nobody as yet, except a few magazine writers, studio attaches, and two stertorous female gossip columnists, has seen. . . .

The fact that Welles is reputed to have incurred the displeasure of an elderly gentleman who doesn't like to have bandied about what he thinks is his biography, is not in itself of great moment. As someone remarked, that is merely a case of juvenile dementia versus senile decay.

The interesting aspect is that an immense industry can be panic stricken by [such] a dispute. . . . Those who are in a position to know say that the heads of the other studios have been enjoined not to permit the picture to be shown in any of the theaters controlled by them, on the penalty that, if they do, whatever dirty linen they are supposed to possess will be brought out and washed in public.

One of the charges that has been festering subcutaneously in the picture business is that of the employment of refugees [from war-torn Europe] to the exclusion of native writers, actors, and technicians. A local trade paper indicated the other day that a threat to expose such alleged practices had been made by the publisher to several studio heads if they did not put the ban on "Citizen Kane."

Whether or not this is true, there is certainly no denying that the whole incident, in addition to

furnishing much amusement, has caused a lot of jitters in the town. . . . Welles met the initial outburst
with a flat denial that there was any intentional sim-
ulation. Since that statement he has refused, pur-
portedly on orders from RKO, to say anything more.

The "threat" to focus on the supposed influx of refu-
gee talent from Europe (Jews, mostly, it meant) being
favored by the studios—most of them run by Jewish
immigrants from an earlier Europe—was not an idle
one. In fact the campaign was actually begun, though
apparently not sustained. Its first shot, a bit surprisingly, was fired by none other than Hearst's good friend
Hedda Hopper (she wrote for non-Hearst papers, giving him a voice in a wider segment of the press). Her
column for January 9 is headed, "FOREIGN ACTORS
CROWDING AMERICANS OFF THE SCREEN."

In the column her comments, carefully calculated as
to how much to state and how far to go, were intended
as a signal, clear if muted, that the "threats" should not
be ignored: "I wonder, in Hollywood's quest for new
faces and its rushing to welcome every new stranger in
our midst, if sometimes it isn't a disadvantage to be an
American. In normal times there's room and opportunity for all. But in times like these, it's like a shoemaker
who makes shoes for everybody else's children and lets
his own go barefoot." Subtly she brings up the case of
two Germans then working in Hollywood, implying
that they were typical examples of the supposed foreign
invasion. Albert Bach, a producer run out of the Reich

by Hitler, she quotes as lamenting that while he himself can't find work in the movie industry, he had brought over a dozen of his friends and relatives, and "they all have good jobs." Concerning a second man she is a bit less subtle:

> In 1940 we've had some fine German actors on the screen. We welcomed Albert Basserman in "Dr. Ehrlich's Magic Bullet." He seemed to give a new meaning to the part because he was the real thing—a German scientist who spoke English poorly. Yet in that same picture we had one of the finest American actresses, Ruth Gordon, who played Mrs. Ehrlich beautifully. Ruth hasn't been seen on the screen since. But Mr. Basserman gave his same perform-ance in "Foreign Correspondent," in "Moon Over Burma," in "Knute Rockne," in "Dispatch From Reuters," and in several others. He also got his wife jobs.

A week after the Hopper column appeared, the *New York Times* returned to the fast-developing story. The assignment this time was handled by one of the few people outside the studio to have actually seen the film, the *Times* Hollywood correspondent, Doug-las Churchill, who had attended the January sneak preview. His story—headlined "ORSON WELLES SCARES HOLLYWOOD"—reports on two new Hearst moves, both of them with a potential for doing extensive, indeed fatal damage. Interestingly, one reached all the way to Washington and into the senate chamber.

The ten-day controversy whirling around possible suppression of the movie, wrote Churchill, was quickly becoming "one of the most serious disputes in Hollywood's turbulent history." Judging by good and substantial evidence,

> the town is threatened with embarrassing publicity unless the picture is withdrawn by RKO. . . . While the Vine Street boys are laying two-to-one that the $800,000 effort will not be released, RKO and Mr. Welles stoutly declare that it will be unveiled on schedule in mid-February, probably at Radio City Music Hall. . . .
>
> Representations [have been] made to Louis B. Mayer of Metro and Harry Warner of Warner Brothers, who are interested in two of the nation's largest theater chains [to deny RKO the use of their hundreds of theaters around the country, is implied].
>
> Other representations of the publisher began an investigation of the alien situation in Hollywood, something about which the industry is most sensitive. In making their inquiries they explained that the information was being gathered for Mr. Hearst's personal use. . . . Hollywood's apprehension is based on the knowledge of its vulnerability. A rip-snorting newspaper Americanization campaign could prove embarrassing. A Congressional investigation, hinted at by Senator Burton K. Wheeler on Monday, might be disastrous. Those outside of RKO are aware of the possibilities, and if they regard them as serious enough they may align themselves with those who think it inadvisable to release "Citizen Kane." It is impossible for a studio to operate without the

cooperation of the other lots and such influence may
be accepted by RKO.

But on the other hand, adds Churchill, RKO had
sunk almost a million dollars into the picture, which
had to be accounted for to stockholders, and there was
always the possibility of lawsuits if the film were to be
released. "If the trouble becomes more acute, Welles'
film career may be ended."

The political angle attempted by Hearst through
Senator Wheeler of Montana was brief and apparently went nowhere, for nothing further is heard of
the senator in this regard. (Wheeler did at this same
time charge Hollywood with making "propaganda
pictures," meaning anti-fascist, intended to draw America into the war. That this was part of Hearst's plan is
doubtful, though it might have been, the multi-
pronged attack taking some weird bounces).

Suddenly and strongly increasing the tension just at
this point was an apparently revealing article in a small,
short-lived magazine called *Friday*. In an underhanded,
Hearst-like ploy it published a photo-layout using a
half-dozen stills from the movie in which was offered
an explicit, point-by-point comparison with Hearst's
life. The accompanying text gave the impression that
the writer had seen the film and knew its background.
"There was only one copy of the script," mistakenly
claimed the story in emphasizing the secrecy of the
closed sets. "Orson wrote it and has been sleeping with

Marion Davies with William Randolph Hearst at about the time of his efforts to kill *Citizen Kane*.

Hearst is questioned by a U.S. Senate committee about a series of forged documents that appeared in his newspapers.

it under his pillow." But no one from the magazine had been anywhere near the picture. The photos were taken from a publicity package sent to the media by Drake.

The behind-the-scenes approach reported by the *Times* as being made to a pair of top studio executives, MGM's Louis Mayer and Warner Brothers' Harry Warner, proved to be far more effective than vague threats about wholesale retribution. Those two together controlled a large portion of America's movie theaters, necessary outlets which, if denied to *Kane,* would effectively cripple it. That approach in fact—with both the Fox and the Loew's chains soon quietly joining in—is what finally led the RKO board to surrender, but temporarily, as they assured Welles and others.

RKO's own theaters numbered fewer than five hundred. The boycott by the other studios, of course not talked about in public as such, cut to much less than half the usual number available. When late in January word reached Schaeffer's office that Radio City Music Hall in New York City, planned for *Kane*'s gala opening, had also canceled the booking—a result of some fierce if veiled outside pressure—he knew he had to call a halt.

Less than two weeks before its announced premier, set for February 14, Schaeffer told reporters that, pending a review of the situation, the date of *Kane*'s release was officially postponed. When a new date was set he would announce it.

❀

Through the January hullabaloo, Orson Welles remained his normal, assured self. Smilingly he brushed aside all predictions of doom, saying how grateful he was to Hearst for the free publicity, and insisting that *Citizen Kane* would open in New York as scheduled. Now, however, with the postponement a publicly admitted fact, he felt considerably sobered. Could the unexpected delay be a prelude to abandonment? In sudden fear he faced the possibility that his plans might after all go wrong, a sensation wholly foreign to his youthfully buoyant spirit. It shocked him into a brazen effort to deny what was incontrovertibly true, that his film was about the tycoon Hearst and no other. Now he claimed that *nothing* of Hearst was in the picture, nothing whatsoever.

In its way, the statement he released to the press in mid-March was a remarkable performance, deftly twisting the reality to its opposite. For the moment he made it seem almost plausible.

Carefully reasoned, his lengthy statement tried to show how the character of Charles Foster Kane had been conceived as a coldly calculated intellectual exercise, without reference to any living person. In this he was of course banking on the likelihood that no one would bother to check and compare his sources in Huxley and in the Hearst biographies. No one did, not much, not enough.

(Hearst and his followers, naturally, knew very well where *Kane* came from, but it was hardly in Hearst's interests to pursue that angle too closely. It wouldn't do for them to demonstrate how the Welles and Mankiewicz script had used the damningly documented facts supplied by Lundberg and Carlson and Bates. To prevail, Hearst had to mount his campaign of intimidation without getting too specific, by assuming, and letting everyone else assume, the implicit truth of his charges.)

Welles began his curious statement by explaining how his search for a proper subject had been purely mental. He was seeking "not a narrative of action so much as an examination of character. For this I desired a man of many sides and many aspects." He would, he decided, depict several people offering divergent opinions about the man, but soon saw that "such a notion could not be worked out if it applied to an ordinary American citizen. I immediately decided that my character should be a public man—an extremely public man—an extremely important one." After much search and study, "he could find no other position in public life besides that of a publisher in which a man of enormous wealth exercises what might be called real power in a democracy."

A mere industrialist, some corporate giant, wouldn't do for the part, he explains, because "no industrialist can ever achieve in a democratic government the kind of general and catholic power with which I wished to invest my particular character. The only solution seemed to be to place my man in charge of some important channel of communication—radio or newspaper."

But since the character, as Welles saw it, had to be elderly and also dead at the start of the movie, "this immediately precluded radio." (Nimble reasoning indeed, even if a shade too clever-seeming.)

With that it became unavoidable that Kane must be "a newspaper publisher, owner of a great chain of newspapers," and from that decision necessarily arose another, that "the history of the newspaper business demanded [!] that Kane be what is generally referred to as a yellow journalist." (Hardly *demanded*. But he slips it by.)

Now he had his "character," in the making of which the image of Hearst had played no least part. How did it happen that this imagined character's career so much resembled that of the man on whom he was *not* modeled? For the verbally agile Welles that was no problem.

Many movies had been based on the formula of a "success story," in which a subject works his way up from lowly beginnings. Welles would do something different. He would do a "failure story," which meant that he had to invest his character "with sixty million dollars at the age of eight so there was no considerable or important gain in point of wealth possible from a dramatic point of view." Thus his story was not about how a man gets money, "but what he does with his money. . . . A man who has money and doesn't have to concern himself with making more, naturally wishes to use it for the sake of power."

Giving Kane a flamboyant, vigorous personality made it urgent that he also exhibit a tendency to a ruthless use of power—so much was "obvious in his makeup." Always the character was engaged in a mad attempt to impose his own will:

> If I had determined to make a motion picture about the life of a great manufacturer of automobiles, I should have found not long after I started writing that my invention occasionally paralleled history itself. The same is true in the case of my fictitious publisher. He was a yellow journalist. He was functioning as such in the great early days of the development of yellow journalism. Self-evidently it was impossible for me to ignore American history. [No, not really impossible, and that word "great," in that context, does seem rather a slip. But let him go on].
>
> I declined to fabricate an impossible or psychologically untrue reaction to American historical events by an American yellow journalist. . . . My picture could not begin the career of such a man in 1890 and take it to 1940 without presenting the man with the same problems which presented themselves to his equivalents in real life. His dealings with these events were determined by dramaturgical and psychological laws which I recognize to be absolute. They were not colored by the facts in history.

Not colored by the facts of *Hearst's* history, he means, saying it without trace of a smile, but only by the "laws" of the drama. His concluding sentence here required considerable nerve to put down on paper but is pure Welles: "The facts in history were actually determined by the same laws which I had always employed as a dramatist."

His sorest problem was to explain away the undeniable resemblance to Hearst in the matter of Kane's blind and unbridled grab for the world's art treasures. He does it by finally throwing logic to the winds, reasoning *from* the fact of the little boy's sled whose brand name provides the word Rosebud. It was solely to account for this sled, says Welles, that he dreamed up *both* Kane's wild collecting habits and the fabulous hilltop castle where he kept his treasures. To house all those bulky if priceless antiques *some* sort of remarkable structure was needed:

> In his waking hours Kane had certainly forgotten the sled and the name which was painted on it. Case books of psychiatrists are full of these stories. It was important for me in the picture to tell the audience as effectively as possible what this really meant. Clearly it would be undramatic and disappointing if an arbitrary character in the story popped up with the information. The best solution was the sled itself. Now, how could this sled still exist since it was built in 1880? It was necessary that my character be a collector—the kind of man who never throws anything away. I wished to use as a symbol—at the conclusion of the picture—a great expanse of objects—thousands and thousands of things—one of which is "Rosebud." This field of inanimate theatrical properties I wished to represent the very dustheap of a man's

life. I wished the camera to show beautiful things, ugly things and useless things, too—indeed everything which could stand for a public career and a private life. . . . There was no way for me to do this except to make my character, as I have said, a collector, and to give him a great house in which to keep his collections. The house itself occurred to me as a literal translation in terms of drama of the expression "ivory tower." The protagonist of my "failure story" must retreat from a democracy which his money fails to buy and his power fails to control. There are two retreats possible: *death* and the *womb*. The house was the womb. Here too was all the grandeur, all the despotism which my man found lacking in the outside world. Such was his estate—such was the obvious repository for a collection large enough to include, without straining the credulity of the audience—a little toy from the dead past of a great man.

In March, through the RKO legal offices, the statement was released to the press. Most papers carried portions of it, paraphrasing the rest.

Not one word of it was true.

7

Waters Rising

At the head of a massive oak table, its mottled surface richly glowing, sat William Randolph Hearst. Crowded round with subordinates, the table stood at one end of the sumptuous Hearst office on the second floor of San Simeon's main building.

The date was early February 1941, and the meeting's business centered on Orson Welles and George Schaeffer. By now Hearst had viewed the movie—in a print probably acquired by means of some back-door maneuvering through his allies at either MGM or Warners—and he had turned it over to his legal department for a detailed analysis.

Now that the picture's public debut had been halted, said Hearst to the assembled group, something must be done about Welles himself. How could the irksome young showman be neutralized, personally discredited, his movie career ended? With *Kane*'s originator and star out of the way for good, the resilient Schaeffer might not be so ready to return to the fight. By now it was clear to Hearst that the RKO president was the main obstacle to the studio's complete surrender, promptly checking every tendency of its board in that direction.

Then, added Hearst, with Welles and his protector brushed aside, it would only be a matter of seeing that the picture was acquired and destroyed, the negative with all its various prints. No trace of the movie would survive but the few publicity stills already issued. It would of course, entail a huge financial loss for RKO—the cost of making the picture plus salaries, advertising, and lost profits. A payment of up to a million in total would be acceptable to him, announced Hearst unconcernedly.

How to get at Welles presented a problem, reported an aide, there being no real opening that they could find just then, aside possibly from his draft status. America's first peacetime draft, prompted by events in Europe, had begun the previous November, and by early 1941 all Hollywood was anxiously waiting to see how it would affect its male stars. Welles had received a high call-up number, so wouldn't be tapped until the spring. Meantime, Hearst operatives were assigned to keep watch on developments in that area, doing what they could to hasten or assure Welles' induction into uniform. As it turned out, his physical condition by itself decided the matter, a fact announced by *Photoplay*

magazine (just after release of *Kane*). An article dar-
ingly titled "The Truth about the Draft in Hollywood"
reported at length on the status of some of the bigger
names, among them Jimmy Stewart, Tyrone Power,
William Holden, Glenn Ford, and Fred MacMurray.
The case of Orson Welles, it explained,

> has been watched with a good deal of interest. After
> two and a half years of being on the Hollywood fir-
> ing line, where he good-naturedly bore the jibes of
> filmdom's bigwigs, he has now come into his own as
> the genius of "Citizen Kane," just released. Among
> the bids for his services pouring in from all the stu-
> dios, he received an inconspicuous invitation with a
> government stamp which took precedence over all
> others.
>
> There was a possibility of his being deferred.
> Welles supports his three-year-old child, who is in the
> custody of his former wife, since remarried, and up to
> the time his picture was actually shown he was virtu-
> ally broke. . . . However, Citizen Kane is not destined
> to become Private Welles, at least not for a while. His
> physical examination disclosed an asthmatic condi-
> tion and Uncle Sam has rated him in the 1-B class.

More was wrong with him than *Photoplay* reported,
however, chronic ailments that during the course of the
war would keep him permanently a civilian: flat feet, a
slight curvature of the spine, and a more serious condition of spina bifida.

In addition to monitoring Welles' draft situation,
Hearst's agents were also set to doing some quiet

investigation on both coasts, among theater people and the film crowd. Something usable would turn up on his personal life, all felt, especially regarding his rumored off-stage activities among the crop of starlets. Given a few promising facts, no matter how tentative, they'd be able to spin out a tidy little scandal—old stuff for Hearst provocateurs. Aside from women, it was assumed, Welles *must* have made a few other missteps during his six-year rise in the New York theater and radio world.

Meantime, instructed the angry Chief, they could start on RKO's head, George Schaeffer.

At that instant, it seemed, the RKO president was locked in a contract dispute with a producer who was alleging bad faith and personal difficulties because of RKO's failure to make his scheduled movie. In a suit in Los Angeles court, just filed, the producer was charging the studio, and Schaeffer in particular, with arbitrary and contrived delay, and was asking damages of over a million dollars. It was, more or less, business as usual in the movie world, and the papers had taken little notice of the so-far subdued legal fight. Not much for Hearst's men to go on, but it would have to do until something juicier came along. At least it would serve notice on the RKO boss that *he* was now in Hearst's sights.

No time was wasted. Within days of the strategy meeting at San Simeon orders went out to all Hearst papers across the country to play the Schaeffer story *big*. All did so, featuring full accounts of the lawsuit, many front-paging it. Multi-column headlines far in excess of the story's importance told of RKO's, but especially Schaeffer's, delinquency. "CHARGES THAT RKO BROKE CONTRACT," was the banner headline used in the *Milwaukee Sentinel*. The story didn't take, however, fizzling when the suit was quickly decided, and in favor of the complaining producer, whose award had dwindled to seven thousand dollars.

Schaeffer, unintimidated, determined to fight to the last even as serious opposition built within the upper ranks at RKO, went steadily about the business of marshaling outside support for *Citizen Kane*. In private theaters on both coasts he arranged to show the picture by special invitation to selected audiences of influential writers, actors, other movie and theater people, and assorted cultural leaders. After a half-dozen such private screenings during March, he succeeded in gathering a highly vocal group of advocates, all of them ready to swear to *Kane*'s status as an authentic masterpiece, a great motion picture which *must* be allowed to live. Gradually through various newspapers and magazines there spread articles praising *Kane* and calling for its immediate release. One particularly effective piece was contributed by prominent novelist John O'Hara (*Appointment in Samarra, Butterfield 8,* etc.). It appeared in *Newsweek* magazine:

> It is with exceeding regret that your faithful bystander reports that he has just seen a picture which he thinks must be the best picture he ever saw. With

Hearst's baronial office at San Simeon. Sitting around this table with his large staff of writers, editors, and undercover operatives he planned his revenge on Orson Welles.

no less regret he reports that he has just seen the best actor in the history of acting.

Name of picture: *Citizen Kane*

Name of actor: Orson Welles

Reason for regret: you, my dear reader, may never see the picture [because it] is rumored to have something to do with a certain publisher who for the first, or maybe the second time in his life, shall be nameless. . . .

A fresh punk out of various colleges, the publisher walks into a newspaper office as a not quite legitimate heir, and thereupon enjoys himself [wielding] power. At a rather late date it is shown that his sybaritic pastimes and his power are incomplete, for he can buy or produce everything but love. . . .

Look in vain here for any but obscure hints as to the story of *Citizen Kane*. My intention is to make you want to see the picture, if possible to make you wonder *why* you are not seeing what I think is as good a picture as was ever made. . . .

I say if you plan to have any grandchildren to bore, see Orson Welles so that you can bore them with some honesty. Do yourself a favor. Go to your neighborhood exhibitor and ask him why he isn't showing *Citizen Kane*.

From *Time* magazine a few days later came similar favorable comment, also lamenting what seemed the impending doom of the film. "As in some grotesque fable," began the piece, "it appeared last week that Hollywood was about to turn upon and destroy its greatest creation. . . . The objection of Mr. Hearst who founded a publishing empire on sensationalism, is ironic. For to most of the several hundred people who have seen the film at private showings, *Citizen Kane* is the most sensational product of the U.S. movie industry. It has found important new techniques in picture-making and storytelling. So sharply does *Citizen Kane* veer from cinema cliché, it hardly seems like a movie."

When Welles first went west nearly two years before, concluded *Time,* Hollywood sneered at the boy wonder and expected that he "would break all the rules. Hollywood was right."

Appearing in the same week as the *Time* story, the even more influential *Life* magazine cast an equally ringing vote for salvaging the beleaguered film. On three of its glossy, oversize pages were spread no fewer than ten stills from the movie, showing ten different scenes, all provided with intriguingly descriptive captions. "To a film industry floundering in a rut," explained the brief, eulogistic text, "*Citizen Kane* offers enough new channels to explore for five years to come."

In Hollywood itself the praise was equally loud, though in at least one case offering a sober word of caution, perhaps the first to reach print, as to its possibly *not* appealing to a mass audience. In a long discussion of the picture's innovations, the *Hollywood Reporter,* while judging *Kane* to be a great movie, feared that a general audience "might not think so because they might not understand its technical perfections. . . . How much an audience's ignorance of these facts will discount the actual entertainment we can't tell."

Not until late March were the Hearst forces able to gather ammunition for a personal attack on Welles. Then—hard to believe of such practiced muckrackers—they went so far overboard that in the public mind they were defeated by their own incredible excess. Hearst's old slashing technique for cutting down his opponents, wielded so often in the past with such devastating results, here went badly off the track.

After completing his work on *Kane,* Welles accepted an invitation to do a quick radio assignment, presenting an original, hour-long play on a topic of his own choosing, and taking the lead in it. He was to be one of a dozen or more famous names who at the invitation of CBS would form a loose, temporary group called the Free Company, the aim being a celebration of America and its fundamental democratic values. Unofficial sponsors of the ambitious project were U.S. Attorney General Robert Jackson and U.S. Solicitor General Francis Biddle.

Taking part were such leading literary figures as William Saroyan, Ernest Hemingway, Stephen Vincent Benet, John Steinbeck, Maxwell Anderson, and Robert Sherwood. Acting in the weekly programs, to be aired on Sunday mornings, were such as Franchot Tone, Charles Bickford, Paul Muni, Burgess Meredith, Betty Field, John Garfield, Claire Trevor, Emund Gwen, and

Melvyn Douglas. Also prominently associated with the effort was George M. Cohan.

Welles' contribution, *His Honor, the Mayor,* a modest effort based on a short story by George Ade, aired after the series had been running for two months, its tenth weekly offering. In it a small-town mayor incurs the wrath of many of his townspeople when, reluctantly citing the First Amendment, he permits a fiercely racist group of white supremacists to hold a public meeting in the town. The play was presented on Sunday, April 6, 1941, and no one expected much if any attention to it beyond the moment. But next morning and for days afterward all the Hearst papers carried stories roundly condemning Welles as un-American, a subversive, in fact a communist. In making the charge Hearst managed to hide behind the respectable façade of the American Legion, various excitable officials of which had often been quick to do his bidding.

One large streamer headline in the *Milwaukee Sentinel* spread itself across six columns, with Welles' name prominent in the second tier:

LEGION BLASTS RADIO DRAMA SERIES
AS BOOST TO REDS—ORSON WELLES,
FREE PLAYERS, FACE PROTEST

Radicalism Is Aided by Productions, Is Assertion

Los Angeles, April 12—A wrathful American Legion was up in arms today in California and throughout the nation over a current, coast-to-coast series of

radio plays which the Legion has branded as un-
American and tending to encourage communism
and other subversive groups.

The broadcasts have been produced by The Free
Company, which includes a number of asserted left-
wing writers and actors. Their indignation was
brought to a head by last Sunday's program, a play
written and acted by Orson Welles, and denounced
by Legionnaires as serving and encouraging subversive groups in this country. . . .

The Welles broadcast . . . was declared by the Legionnaires to have been one of the most offensive of
all the broadcasts because they considered it a subtle
form of communistic undermining of American
unity in the present defense situation, an outright
appeal for the right of a subversive fifth column
group to hold anti-American meetings in the public
hall of an American city.

Three days later the *Sentinel* reported that the Legion was demanding a congressional investigation of
both the Free Company and CBS: "The fighting spirit
of the American Legion members demonstrated in the
World War was equaled by their staunch defense of our
democratic ideals that they hold are endangered by the
plays of Orson Welles and his Free Company. . . . If
Orson Welles is connected with the series of broadcasts, there must be some communistic trend in it."
One Legion officer was quoted as calling for an official
crackdown on the offending broadcasters: "The li-
censes of the stations ought to be revoked."

Two days later the *Sentinel*'s attack was renewed. Legion officials in Chicago would make a formal demand that the programs be stopped and an investigation begun. Their resolution "severely criticizes Orson Welles for producing plays designed to discourage the youth of America from believing in the American form of government, but also the Columbia Broadcasting System for permitting these broadcasts."

At first Welles brushed aside the veiled hate campaign as needing no reply, being self-evidently refuted. But two weeks of hammering by the Hearst press got the better of him. In a press statement he frankly named his antagonist and the reason for the attack:

> William Randolph Hearst is conducting a series of brutal attacks on me in his newspapers. It seems he doesn't like my picture *Citizen Kane*. . . . I have stood by silently in the hope that this vicious attack would be spent in the passing of a few weeks. . . . But I can't remain silent any longer.
>
> The Hearst papers have repeatedly described me as a communist. I am not a communist. I am grateful for our constitutional form of government and I rejoice in our great American tradition of democracy. Needless to say, it is not necessarily unpatriotic to disagree with Mr. Hearst.

Not too surprisingly, before long the non-Hearst press came to Welles' defense, one Pittsburgh paper declaring that if Welles was a communist for advocating free speech, "then too is George M. Cohan a communist." In the *New York Times* an editorial made plain the fact that "the campaign against Mr. Welles is more concerned with a motion picture than with radio." In a few brief words the *Chicago Sun Times* placed the whole ugly episode in perspective: "If it weren't sad it would be silly. William Randolph Hearst is piqued with Orson Welles. The rest is camouflage."

Behind the scenes some even uglier attacks on Welles were attempted, and in Hearst's more personally brutal style, or so it appears. One effort in particular is known about only by way of Welles himself—admittedly not the best witness since his memory did tend to embellish and dramatize the past, his own not least. Still, what he recalled in this instance fits so well with the character of the accused, and with what is known otherwise of his anti-*Kane* campaign, that it should at least be put plainly on the record.

During a ten-day period in the early spring of 1941, while the fate of *Kane* hung in the balance, Welles went off on a quick lecture tour arranged by his agent (a way of picking up some interesting money fast). One date was in the east, probably Pittsburgh, and here, claimed Welles, Hearst's operatives actually tried to frame him on a morals charge. The evidence for the attempt is skimpy and indirect, not at all adequate—but then from the nature of the incident it couldn't be.

In a 1951 interview, in talking about *Kane* and Hearst, Welles let drop a tantalizing comment: "Hearst and the people around him did me terrible harm. . . . Some day when I write my autobiography I'll tell of the damage they did me, and the frame-ups they tried."

He never did write his autobiography, and not until forty years went by did he add anything to that claim of "frame-up." Even then the information came out not quite deliberately but almost in passing. During another interview about the movie, this one is 1982, the conversation at one point suddenly veered around to Hearst. Without being asked a specific question on the point, Welles abruptly volunteered:

> They were really after me. I was lecturing—I think it was Pittsburgh, some town like that—and a detective came up to me as I was having supper with some friends after the lecture. He said, don't go back to your hotel. I'm from police headquarters. . . . I said why not? He said, I'm just giving you advice. I said, what are you talking about? He said, they've got a fourteen-year-old girl in the closet and two cameramen waiting for you to come in. And of course I would have gone to jail. There would have been no way out of it.
>
> I never went back to the hotel. I just waited till the train in the morning. I've often wondered what happened to the cameramen and the girl waiting all night for me to arrive.

At first blush the story does seem unlikely, a little drama that Welles had built up over the years from some casual incident or suggestive remark he'd overheard (his exaggerations always needed hard fact of some kind as a stimulus). That feeling of uncertainty and doubt, however, fades fast away for anyone at all familiar with the multitude of similar shocking transgressions practiced by Hearst and his newspapers over the decades. Welles that night in Pittsburgh may well, as he was convinced, have barely escaped a plot to put him away and destroy his reputation.

As it happened, at the very time of the Free Company imbroglio Welles was enjoying renewed attention for another of his incarnations, that of a theatrical director. Through February and most of March he had been in New York City staging a new play, *Native Son* (adapted by Paul Green from the best-selling novel by Richard Wright). Responding to an invitation from John Houseman, who owned the property, grateful to be again working in the legitimate theater where he could for a time forget his troubles over *Kane,* he had put in six grueling weeks of fifteen-hour days shaping the difficult material. Opening on March 24 in the St. James Theater on Broadway, the play proved an immediate hit, with the major credit going to Welles' inspired direction. Critic after critic identified Welles' part as crucial and reviews of the first night were all raves. Singled out as pivotal were Welles' "dynamic use of the stage," echoing what had been said of his work on *Kane,* that its groundbreaking style made other movies seem old-fashioned. "It is as if the theater had been shaken up and recharged with new life," ventured one bemused reviewer of *Native Son.* "The theater, that slumbering giant, tears off its chains in this production," said another. Beyond all doubt, said a third, "Orson Welles is the greatest theatrical director of the modern stage."

All the way from California came several critics to attend *Native Son*'s debut, an unusual move for the day. One of these was John Hobart of the *San Francisco Chronicle,* a Hearst rival, who filed something more than a mere rave:

> The kid has done it again. Chubby-faced Orson Welles, the boy genius, not content with such feats as his Man from Mars broadcast which frightened the entire nation a few years ago, and *Citizen Kane* which has intimidated the entire movie industry, is now whipping Gotham into a lather of excitement with his latest stage production.
>
> At the moment all New York seems to be gabbling heatedly about *Native Son,* which opened at the St. James Monday night. It is a high-voltage melodrama. . . . [It is] dynamite that sets off explosions inside you. . . . If the staging were less extraordinary it might not seem quite so sensational. . . . It played without an intermission. . . . The scenes are acted at various levels within a framework of yellow brick wall. . . . The lighting is brilliantly managed, for the play moves in continually shifting pools of light. . . . It was one of Broadway's more spectacular openings.

By mid-April, Welles—still a month from his twenty-sixth birthday—had become the best-known, most extravagantly praised theatrical personality in the English-speaking world. In many European capitals, also, his was the best-known American theatrical name. It was now that George Schaeffer, taking at its flood the rising tide of public attention, made his fateful move in regard to the suspended *Citizen Kane*.

❀

Sitting around a long table in the RKO boardroom were the company's seven directors. Alternately they were listening to, then questioning, the firm's president, who occupied a chair at the table's head. Handling the questions, Schaeffer displayed an easy confidence he didn't really feel, not entirely.

Compelling everyone's attention at the moment was a single urgent topic: if *Kane* were to be released, would it be sure to benefit RKO? Would it earn a decent profit and add to the company's reputation for excellence? Or would it bring down on them more trouble than it was worth, legal and otherwise? As it proved in the resulting discussion, the problem had many angles, one of which even touched on the film's artistic worth.

For this moment, the first major crisis of his career as a film executive, Schaeffer had prepared himself well. To start, he said to the listening members, the RKO lawyers had carefully reviewed the picture in the light of the state's libel and invasion of privacy laws. They were satisfied that if several stray references in the movie were removed—a matter of less than three minutes' running time—there was small likelihood of a lawsuit by Hearst, almost none. The offending minutes, he added, were out, they'd already been cut. If the truculent Hearst did make the mistake of bringing suit he couldn't possibly win—

A voice: Why not?

First he'd have to establish legal proof that *Kane* was in fact a portrait of him, a deliberate portrait. That is far harder to do than simply pointing out similarities. The law is strict and very specific when it comes to proving identity. Nothing fuzzy will do. Then ask yourself this. Would Hearst really *want* to pile up proofs that the damning things said about Kane were true of *him* in real life? To have any sort of case he'd have to do just that.

As for possible profits—here Schaeffer couldn't keep from smiling broadly—*never* had a movie made its debut with such a fanfare of publicity! Nationwide. Money couldn't buy its equivalent. News of the fight with Hearst had reached into every corner of the country, from the big cities to the sleepiest small towns, carried by newspapers, magazines, and radio. Along with reports of the heated quarrel went all those critical raves about the picture, hailing *Kane* as fascinatingly different, a new kind of movie. People would *flock* to see it!

Think of all those professionals who've seen the picture in private and who have absolutely raved about it. Leading directors, actors, big-name producers, honored literary figures, and whatnot, all of them *demanding* that *Kane* be released!

Gentlemen, ventured Schaeffer, with *Citizen Kane* we'll have the highest grossing movie in history. And the highest net! A profit way up in the millions, our stats man says, a return of four or five hundred percent, or even more, depending.

A voice: But the theater boycott by the chains, what about that? How can a movie survive losing all those outlets, MGM and Fox and the others? How do we make up that shortfall in attendance, and if we don't, where do the millions come from? If an audience can't see a film where they live, what good is free publicity?

Schaeffer was prepared for the question. They'll never do it, he replied confidently. It's all a bluff. If they do try it, our legal department is set to bring suit. It'd be a conspiracy in restraint of trade. We'd sue and we'd win. Hearst's people know that. We've talked with them.

A voice: You sound sure of yourself, George. You just talking or *are* you sure?

Gentlemen, I can tell you there's no fear of a shutdown. This isn't the 1890s. Hearst isn't *that* powerful anymore. He couldn't start a war today the way he did back then. Even if we lose a few houses we'll still reach the audience OK. And there's this: Hearst's threat to lock us out through his friends denying us their theaters is *good* for us! More publicity! We've reached the point where every piece of skullduggery they try against the picture helps us! Anyway, you think those chains will turn their backs on the kind of business *Kane* will generate for them?

A voice: That means you're definite about refusing Mayer's offer to buy the picture from us? We shouldn't even consider accepting the eight hundred grand and being safe? Why not talk it over with them? Hearst might raise the total to include a profit percentage. All he's offering now is what we spent. He knows it'll take more than that to get his hands on the picture so he can destroy it.

Schaeffer burst out laughing. Now *that,* he said emphatically, was their final big mistake! Sending an offer like that through Louis to buy *Kane*! Who wouldn't be dying to see a movie that the great William R. Hearst would go so far and pay so much to kill? What movie fan could stay away once he heard *that* juicy bit? Believe me, we'll play that angle for all its worth in the papers. *Variety* broke the story a month ago so it's already going around. The highest gross and net *ever,* I'm telling you!

A voice (friendly, the speaker smiling): George, tell us the truth. Those threats Orson made in public last month about suing us for damages if we canceled or sold the picture. Did he mean it? Was it something you two cooked up to spook this board? Come on, the truth.

Schaeffer, pausing, returned the smile. Now do you really think, he asked evenly, that I, your faithful servant, would ever, ever stoop to such artifice. . . .

A voice: If it was a trick he carried it pretty far. Called a press conference at his hotel in New York and gave out a statement demanding that we set a release date or he'd sue. Here it is in the *Motion Picture Herald,* part of it anyway. Sounds pretty sure of himself. Listen to this:

For me to stand by while this picture was being suppressed would constitute a breach of faith on my part as a producer. I have at this moment sufficient financial backing to buy *Citizen Kane* from RKO and release it myself. Under my contract with RKO I have the right to demand that the picture be released, and to bring legal action to force its release if necessary. RKO *must* release *Citizen Kane*. If it does not do so immediately I have instructed my attorney to commence proceedings. . . . Any such attempts at suppression would involve a serious interference with freedom of speech and with the integrity of the motion picture industry as the foremost medium of expression in the country. . . . I regret exceedingly that anyone should interpret *Citizen Kane* as having a bearing upon any living person, or should impugn the artistic purposes of its producers.

Sounds to me like he means business. Does he really have the backing to buy the picture from us? Where would he get hold of a million dollars? As I hear it he's mostly broke or close to it, waiting for his next big payday!

Schaeffer smiled. Who knows where he'd get it? Somebody said maybe from Henry Luce at *Time*. Luce is no friend of Hearst. Says he'd show it in *tents*! At circuses!

A voice: What about him suing?

That's Orson for you, replied Schaeffer. He cited his contract which he says gives him a clear proprietary interest in the picture. It may or may not—the contract does allow him a share of the profits. Myself, I wouldn't want to test it.

A voice: OK, George, say everything goes right for us. Say Hearst backs off. Doesn't sue, doesn't get his friends at the other studios lined up against us. We're home free. What about the picture itself? I've heard and read some things about it being the kind of movie that gets lots of terrific reviews, then plays to empty seats. You've heard it, we've all heard it.

Schaeffer shook his head. Yes, I've heard it, he replied evenly, and I'll be honest. Sure some people will rather spend their money on belly-laughs, and tear-jerkers, and shoot-em-up stuff. But it won't matter. We'll still have most of the market or a big share of it, a *big* share. Don't forget what I just told you. We're riding the most stupendous wave of movie publicity ever to come out of this town, a drumbeat you couldn't *buy*!

On April 9 the RKO publicity staff issued a bulletin, requesting immediate pickup by all media. *Citizen Kane,* it announced, would open on May 1 in New York City. The site would be RKO's own Palace Theater at Forty-seventh Street and Broadway. An old house—its heyday had come in the days of vaudeville—much smaller than Radio City Music Hall, which was still unavailable, the Palace would get a facelift for the occasion. The refurbished old theater, said the release, would be made into a properly magnificent setting for the debut of the world's greatest movie.

8

Flood Tide

To play the Palace.

For decades up through the 1920s, until the movies took over, that had been the dream of every halfway decent vaudeville act. Across the capacious stage of New York's Palace Theater had passed thousands of name performers, including every headliner from Lillian Russell, Harry Lauder, and Elsie Janis, "The Sweetheart of the AEF," to Cohan, Jolson, and Eva Tanguay, the "I-Don't-Care Girl." Now, in the spring of 1941, occupying the old building would be the ultimate example of the kind of entertainment that had, a bare eight years before, run those old troupers off the stage for good.

The ten-story building whose lower floors housed the Palace hadn't changed much. The most obvious difference could be seen down near street level, where a thick, square marquee hanging from the classical stone façade jutted out over the sidewalk. Now, in the last days of April, on each of its three sides, spelled out in six-foot-high letters, passersby could read the title of the next attraction, set to premier on May 1, and the name of its creator:

ORSON WELLES
CITIZEN KANE

Stretching high above the marquee was a vertical billboard thirty feet tall affixed to the building's narrow front. It showed the illuminated figure of Orson Welles, in black trousers and a white shirt open at the neck, the figure nine times repeated, one behind the other, at each repetition growing larger, arms gradually extended and raised until the last figure stands in a triumphal pose. The apparent movement is emphasized by the illumination outlining each successive image which jumps upward from figure to figure. Over and around the whole assemblage concealed jets periodically release steam to billow mysteriously.

Across the top of the billboard, above the head of the last Welles figure, are only two words in huge lettering:

IT'S TERRIFIC!

Above the billboard, formed by separate letters each eight feet high, easily read a mile off, Welles' name was again proclaimed. Only his name, nothing more.

It is seven P.M. on May 1. The announced starting time of the movie is 8:30, and as the newspaper ads stated all seats were priced at $2.20. Thereafter, evening prices would be $1.10, $1.65, and $2.20. Weekday matinee prices started at 75 cents, Saturdays and Sundays at 85 cents.

A weeklong ad campaign costing $50,000 has spread word of the premier to every corner of New York City's five boroughs, reaching as well into neighboring New Jersey and Connecticut. Beneath the marquee, now brilliantly lighted, a milling mob of men and women crowds the theater entrance and the sidewalk for a hundred yards in either direction. A line of policemen keeps people from spilling out onto the street, allowing a steady stream of cars, taxis, and limousines to pull up at the entrance. Whenever a familiar face emerges from an opening door a murmur runs through the crowd: That's John Garfield! Look there's Kate Smith! Oh, it's Eleanor Powell!

Almost every name actor from every play on Broadway has shown up, as well as a contingent of Hollywood stars and the leaders of New York's café society. Sprinkled through the noisy audience are some three dozen eager film critics. For all who enter there is a souvenir program, a glossy, twenty-eight-page booklet extoling both Welles and the film. "The amazing Mr. Welles," he is called in its opening pages, and "man of endless surprises." A two-page spread highlights his many talents, naming him "The Four-most Personality of Motion Pictures" (author, producer, director, star). No fewer than eighteen photographs show Welles as himself, while another twenty show him as Kane.

Just before starting time a limousine pulls to a stop at the theater entrance and out steps Orson Welles, his tall figure dapper in a tuxedo, his appearance sending a ripple of excitement through the mob. Turning, Welles offers a hand to his companion, the beautiful Dolores Del Rio, dazzling in a feathery white gown.

Stopping briefly at the doorway to be interviewed for radio, the two wave to the cheering crowd and go inside. Instead of taking their seats, however, they veer right, go up a short staircase and slip quietly into the office of the theater manager, who welcomes them warmly. There they stay until the film begins. Then led by the manager they go down a back stairway to a private exit door, walk quickly through an alleyway, and come out on a side street where a taxi waits. Five minutes later they are back in their separate rooms at the Ambassador.

Earlier, Welles had informed Schaeffer and the other RKO officials that, once he'd made his entrance, he'd disappear. Sitting and watching his maiden film unfold on a huge screen before a live audience was a situation, he explained, that he just couldn't stand—knowing he could no longer change anything! With his stage plays, whether as actor-director or director only, even after opening night he never stopped tinkering, making small adjustments even as the play ran, whether it was a hit or not. *Citizen Kane* was now out of his control, beyond improving, at least for a while, at least in any major way. Watching it run in a crowded theater would simply be too hard on the nerves.

Blocked by Hearst from opening *Citizen Kane* at New York's Radio City Music Hall, the picture had its May 1941 premier at New York's old Palace Theater.

At the hotel desk he'd left orders to have all the city's morning papers delivered to his room as soon as they hit the streets. That night he didn't sleep well, so it was in some relief that, a little after six A.M., he heard a knock at the door. The uniformed page handed him a neat bundle of papers that included the *Sun,* the *Post,* the *Times,* the *World-Telegram,* the *Herald Tribune,* the *News,* and the *Mirror.*

It was the *Times,* the country's most influential paper, that he opened first, standing in the middle of the room and dropping the other papers to the floor. Flipping the pages he quickly found the review, prominent in the top, left corner of page ten. It was by Bosley Crowther, a long-established critic of formidable reputation. His eyes racing, Welles read every word of the column-long text:

> Within the withering spotlight as no other film has ever been before, Orson Welles' "Citizen Kane" had its world premier at the Palace last evening. And now that the wraps are off, the mystery has been exposed and Mr. Welles and the RKO directors have taken the much-debated leap, it can be safely stated that the suppression of this film would have been a crime.
>
> In spite of some disconcerting lapses and strange ambiguities in the creation of the principal character, "Citizen Kane" is far and away the most surprising and cinematically exciting motion picture to be seen here in many a moon. As a matter of fact, it comes close to being the most sensational film ever made in Hollywood.

Count on Mr. Welles: he doesn't do things by halves. Being a mercurial fellow with a frightening theatrical flair, he moved right into the movies, grabbed the medium by the ears, and began to toss it around with the dexterity of a seasoned veteran. Fact is, he handled it with more verve and inspired ingenuity than any of the elder craftsmen have exhibited in years.

With the able assistance of Gregg Toland, whose services should not be overlooked, he found in the camera the perfect instrument to encompass his dramatic energies and absorb his prolific ideas. Upon the screen he discovered an area large enough for his expansive whims to have free play. And the consequence is that he has made a picture of tremendous and overpowering scope, not in physical extent so much as in its rapid and graphic rotation of thought.

Mr. Welles has put upon the screen a motion picture that really moves.

As for the story which he tells—and which has provoked such an uncommon fuss—this corner frankly holds considerable reservation. Naturally we wouldn't know how closely—if at all—it parallels the life of an eminent publisher, as has been somewhat cryptically alleged. But that is beside the point in a rigidly critical appraisal. The blamable circumstance is that it fails to provide a clear picture of the character and motives behind the man about whom the whole thing revolves.

As the picture opens Charles Kane lies dying in the fabulous castle he has built—the castle called Xanadu, in which he has surrounded himself with vast treasures. And as death closes his eyes his heavy lips murmur one word, "Rosebud." Suddenly the death scene is broken; the screen becomes alive with a staccato March-of-Time-like news feature recounting the career of the dead man—how as a poor boy he came into great wealth, how he became a newspaper publisher as a young man, how he aspired to political office, was defeated because of a personal scandal, devoted himself to material acquisition, and finally died.

But the editor of the news feature is not satisfied; he wants to know the secret of Kane's strange nature and especially what he meant by "Rosebud." So a reporter is dispatched to find out, and the remainder of the picture is devoted to an absorbing visualization of Kane's phenomenal career as told by his boyhood guardian, two of his closest newspaper associates, and his mistress. Each is agreed on one thing—that Kane was a titanic egomaniac.

It is also clearly revealed that the man was in some way consumed by his own terrifying selfishness. But just exactly what it is that eats upon him, why it is there and, for that matter, whether Kane is really a villain, a social parasite, is never clearly revealed. And the final, poignant identification of "Rosebud" sheds little more than a vague, sentimental light upon his character. At the end, Kubla Kane is still an enigma—a very confusing one.

But check that off to the absorption of Mr. Welles in more visible details. Like the novelist Thomas Wolfe his abundance of imagery is so great that it sometimes gets in the way of his logic. And the less critical will probably be content with a less defined

Kane anyhow. After all, nobody understands him. Why should Mr. Welles?

Isn't it enough that he presents a theatrical character with consummate theatricality?

We would indeed like to say as many nice things as possible about everything else in this film—about the excellent direction of Mr. Welles, about the sure and penetrating performances of literally every member of the cast, and about the stunning manner in which the music of Bernard Herrmann has been used. Space unfortunately, is short.

All we can say in conclusion is that you shouldn't miss this film. It is cynical, ironic, sometimes oppressive, and as realistic as a slap. But it has more vitality than fifteen other films we could name. And although it may not give a thoroughly clear answer, at least it brings to mind one deeply moral thought: For what shall it profit a man if he shall gain the whole world and lose his own soul? See "Citizen Kane" for further details.

Brushing aside the references to "disconcerting lapses," and the criticism of Kane's faulty portrait, hardly pausing to revel in the ringing praise, Welles reached down and picked up the next paper, this time choosing the sober, prestigious *Post*. Its critic, the lesser known Archer Winsten, adopted the long view, his tone cool and fittingly objective:

Not since Chaplin's *A Woman of Paris* has an American film struck an art and an industry with comparable force. It goes without saying that this is the film that wins the majority of 1941's movie prizes in a walk. It will be important in the history of American motion pictures

Orson Welles with this one film establishes himself as the most exciting director now working. Assiduously avoiding obvious dodges of the arty, he brings a clear, unfettered intelligence to the problems of the sound picture. Technically the result marks a new epoch in movie-making.

Next to be picked up was the *Sun,* but it proved to be curiously distant and even lukewarm. The critic, Eileen Creelman, couldn't muster any enthusiasm at all for the innovative technique, preferring to dwell on the "confusion" noted by Crowther. "An interesting film with a decided personality all its own," she called it. "But it is a cold picture, unemotional, a puzzle rather than a drama. . . . The interest is only intellectual, not dramatic."

The tabloid *Daily News* was better, but brief and curiously restrained: "It is one of the most interesting and technically superior films that has ever come out of a Hollywood studio."

Reaching for New York's other tabloid, the *Daily Mirror,* Welles remembered that it was a Hearst paper. Leafing through it he fully expected to find a furiously damning opinion. There was nothing at all. If the *Mirror* critic had attended the opening he'd written nothing, or else what he wrote had been rejected.

Much more satisfying was the *World-Telegram's* William Boehnel. Taking some pains, he analyzed the film at length, joining the *Post* and the *Times* in their unstinted admiration: "What matters is that *Citizen Kane* is a cinema masterpiece—that here is a film so full of drama, pathos, humor, drive, variety, and courage and originality in its treatment, that it is staggering, and belongs at once among the great screen achievements."

The last paper Welles stooped to pick up from the floor was the *Herald-Tribune,* whose critic, Howard Barnes, was held in equal esteem with Crowther of the *Times*. Sounding a muted note of surprise at how well RKO's gamble had turned out, his review ran longest of all, and offered the most sustained and discerning praise. Interestingly, it found in the characterization of Kane precisely what Bosley Crowther said wasn't there:

> The motion picture stretched its muscles at the Palace Theater last night to remind one that it is the sleeping giant of the arts. A young man named Orson Welles has shaken the medium wide awake with his magnificent film, "Citizen Kane."
>
> His biography of an American dynast is not only a great picture, it is something of a revolutionary screen achievement. From the standpoint of original treatment and technical innovations one has to go back to the "Birth of a Nation" to find its equal. As a starkly compelling entertainment, using all the tricks and artistry of the cinema, it can only be compared with "The Informer."
>
> Welles, after a very brief period of trial-and-error experimentation, has fully mastered the idiom of the photoplay. In "Citizen Kane" he has employed it for

The phrase "It's Terrific!" became the dominant slogan in the *Citizen Kane* publicity campaign during 1941, as is seen in this newspaper ad for the film's San Francisco opening.

a full and rich expression of American life. His talents were not inconsiderable when he was working in the theater. They are triumphant on the screen. . . . In its vivid, realistic treatment, in the extraordinary depth of its characterizations, and the provocative overtones of this personal drama, "Citizen Kane" is as significant as it is experimental and entertaining.

Only in "The Informer" will you find such fully dimensional characters as people this Orson Welles production. From the megalomaniac Kane himself, to the least significant of his retainers, the show is constantly vitalized by real and arresting portrayals. Much credit for this must go to the rather unknown players in the film, including Welles himself, but more is due the scenario, fashioned by the producer-director and Herman J. Mankiewicz, and the brilliant Welles direction. . . .

It is far more than a mere biography. It is a dramatization of human experience as only the screen can dramatize it. And it hangs together as a "movie" so that the cumulative impact of two hours of screen imagery is stunning. . . . As a portrait of a man with a consuming passion for power and possessions, "Citizen Kane" is not always pleasant, but it is always human and frequently sympathetic. . . . From any standpoint it is a great motion picture.

Before noontime that morning after the premier, Welles was handed another paper by the pageboy at the door, the magazinish *PM*. In it, finally, he could read the words of a critic, Cecilia Ager, who had almost literally been bowled over. "It's as if you never saw a

movie before," she wrote. "No movie has ever grabbed
you, pummeled you, socked you on the button [as] this
one does. . . . You feel as if you're swept up in a torrent
of riches, as if in encountering Orson Welles you've
chanced upon an endless current of imagination, vigor,
courage, decision, and incredible competence."

In American theatrical history there can have been
no other moment of sheer gladsome joy to match the
one experienced by the twenty-six-year-old Welles in
his room at the Ambassador on the morning of May 2,
1941. At the Palace Theater six blocks away, he had a
film, his first, being hailed by top professional observ-
ers and critics as stunningly new and revolutionary,
certainly one of the truly great films ever. His own performance as an actor in it was no less saluted, some calling it among the most superb put on film. Two blocks
downtown from the Palace, at the St. James Theater,
his acclaimed production, *Native Son,* was in its fifth
smash week, still running to packed houses.

Then as he basked in the glowing reviews of *Kane* he
answered a knock at the door of his room. There, looking radiant, stood Delores Del Rio, one of the world's
most beautiful women, come to join him for breakfast.

❀

Across the country gleefully hopped the picture as, in
the space of a week, it opened in Chicago, Hollywood,
and Los Angeles, then in another two weeks began
playing in San Francisco, Boston, and Washington.

In Chicago where it opened at two theaters simultaneously, the Woods and the Palace, the New York critical reception was repeated almost exactly. Again the vote was overwhelmingly in favor of *Kane* as a masterpiece "of fabulous screen stature." Again there were those, a minority, who disliked the new techniques and who felt that the picture's "sacrifice of simplicity to eccentricity robs it of distinction and general entertainment value. . . . It runs to gargantuan sets and arty photography, shadowy and spooky. . . . I kept wishing they'd let a little sunshine in."

While still in Chicago, where he'd attended an opening, Welles was handed a copy of the *New Yorker,* the issue for May 3. In it he found the most thoughtful notice of *Kane* yet, written after much obvious reflection by John Mosher, who wasted no time with superlatives:

CHILDE ORSON

The noise and the nonsense that have attended the release of "Citizen Kane" may for the time being befog the merit of this extraordinary film. Too many people may have too ready an inclination to seek out some fancied key in it, after the silly flurry in our press, and to read into the biography of its leading character extraneous resemblances to persons in actual life. . . .

Since movies hitherto have commenced with a cast list and a vast directory of credits, we are promptly jolted out of our seats when "Citizen Kane" ignores this convention and slides at once into its story. For introduction there is only a stylized and atmospheric hint of background, of shut high gates and formidable fencing, and this formal difference seems revolutionary enough to establish Mr. Welles' independence of the conventions. This independence, like fresh air, sweeps on and on throughout the movie, and in spite of bringing to mind, by elaborately fashioned decoration, a picture as old in movie history as "Caligari," the irregularity of the opening sets a seal of original craftsmanship on what follows. Something new has come to the movie world at last.

Mr. Welles is not merely being smart, clever, or different. By the elliptical method he employs he can trace a man's life from boyhood to death, presenting essential details in such brief flashes that we follow a complex narrative simply and clearly, and find an involved and specialized character fully depicted, an important man revealed to us. With a few breakfast scenes, the process of a marriage is shown as specifically as though we had read the wife's diary. . . .

Sometimes I thought there was too much shadow, that the film seemed to be performed in the dark. Mr. Welles likes gloom. He blots out the faces of speakers, and voices come from a limbo when it is what is being said and not how people look that is important. Only once or twice at times like these does the film seem mannered. For the most part we are too absorbed in the story and its characters to observe any tricks, too swiftly carried on by its intense, athletic scenes. . . .

Mr. Kane does not come out of all this a melodrama villain. I think it is a triumph of the film, and proof of its solid value and of the sense of its director and all concerned, that a human touch is not lost. Sympathy for the preposterous Mr. Kane survives. Indeed there is something about him which seems admirable. I can imagine that various rich gentlemen who own newspapers may find the characterization only right and proper, and claim that their sensitivity, like Mr. Kane's, has been misunderstood by their intimates. Others may recognize many a Mr. Kane among their competitors.

Two days after Chicago came Hollywood, where the picture opened at the El Capitan, a theater that had seldom or never shown movies. In an atmosphere of old-style ballyhoo, with bleachers set up across from the entrance for the enthusiastic spectators, and huge searchlights throwing garish beams over and above the scene, arriving celebrities were handed copies of the glossy souvenir booklet and ushered inside after saying a word of greeting into the radio mike. Their number, however, seems to have been lower than expected, leading RKO to suspect Hearst's hidden hand. *Variety* the day before, in fact, had gotten wind of something in the air and wasn't afraid to put it into print. "Motion picture celebs are being bluntly told," it reported, "that they will incur enmity in certain quarters by attending the coast preem Thursday night of *Citizen Kane* at the El Capitan. It is understood that those who disregard the warning will be tabbed by spotters and reported to headquarters."

Just *whose* headquarters wasn't stated, though the obvious implication was Hearst at San Simeon. The item itself, in a paper read by all show people, must have served to warn off any number of stars who might otherwise have gladly attended. (Specifically noticed as being on hand were Charles Laughton, Gloria Swanson, Mickey Rooney, Maureen O'Hara, Franchot Tone, Olivia de'Haviland, Sonia Henie, Bob Hope, Dorothy Lamour, Adolph Menjou, and Anna Nagel.)

Welles himself showed up, again with Dolores Del Rio on his arm, and again the two slipped out a side door after the film began. He still couldn't sit through a screening of his movie without calculating how it might be improved.

The hometown reviews, in the quality and level of their praise, easily matched those of Chicago and New York, while assuming a more professional tone. "Mr. Welles' cinema bomb," wrote the *Los Angeles Times* critic, "exploded last night at the El Capitan Theater. It hit many of the marks intended brilliantly and skillfully." The *Los Angeles Daily News* found that Welles' "jigsaw puzzle portrait of a man is an adult work of art. . . . The free hand that RKO gave Welles in the production of 'Citizen Kane' is responsible for the introduction of something actually new in motion pictures."

The widely read *Hollywood Citizen-News* declared that the picture was "so remarkable a photoplay that it is bound to jar the most placid film-goer out of the comfortable rut which years of Hollywood pictures have grooved for him. . . . It would have been a sorry thing if RKO had withheld the picture from release . . . a sorry thing for the movie industry which would have suffered a setback in its progress toward realization of its fullness as an entertainment medium."

Unlike the earlier openings, no Hollywood critic found anything to blame or censure (aside from one who felt that there might be a few too many "unusual camera angles"). The picture altogether, everyone agreed, was truly "extraordinary," and Welles himself in his multiple roles of producer, director, cowriter, and star, nothing short of "incredible." Also singled out for special mention were Joseph Cotten and Dorothy Commingore, both receiving high praise.

Welles was still in Hollywood, a day or so later, when a note of warning reached him signaling what might be called the start of the still-echoing controversy over *Citizen Kane*'s true artistic worth. The warning was sounded by critic Bosley Crowther in the *New York Times,* whose initial praise of *Kane* had been unstinted. After viewing the movie a second time Crowther was offering some second thoughts, expanding on the hesitation he'd hinted at in his first review.

So many critics, he began, had hailed *Kane* as one of the great movies of all time, maybe even the greatest, that it was necessary to cite and explain a major flaw in it, a flaw which lowered its stature considerably.

Dorothy Commingore
in publicity photos at
the time of Kane's 1941
premier. "She knocked
them cold," said one
typical story, "and be-
came the movie discov-
ery of the year."

News of the picture's link with the notorious Hearst, Crowther pointed out, had spread to all corners of the country, creating "an audience waiting breathless and alert . . . regardless of what the film actually showed on the screen, this extraordinary advance publicity had pre-ordered a mental attitude" of willing expectation. Viewers in general "were prepared to see in *Kane* an archetype of a ruthless publisher" (specifically Hearst, but Crowther avoided naming him). In other words, viewers were reading into the picture more than was actually there:

> Because the real significance of *Kane* depends entirely upon one's perceptions, we are inclined to feel that Mr. Welles is slightly hoodwinking the public. . . . [The movie] reveals Kane as an egomaniac, a colossus who bestrides the world from his poor and humble beginnings to his death in a secluded pleasure-dome. But the enigma of his life is never solved . . . and when the significance of "Rosebud" is made apparent in the final sequence of the film, it provides little more than a dramatic and poignant shock. It does not clarify, except by sentimental suggestion, the reason for Kane's complexity. . . .
>
> And so we are bound to conclude that this picture is not truly great, for its theme is basically vague and its significance depends on circumstances.

The idea Crowther presents is simple—much simpler than his involved expression of it. For his innovative film, in a word, Welles had picked a story that was not worth the telling. It was the old familiar story of one man's greed and self-love. Without an extra, life-giving dimension it wasn't worth lingering over. Welles' mistake was in tying himself so rigidly to Hearst.

So far, it can be argued, Crowther was exactly right. Kane, basically, *is* a stock figure, and the film's cursory portrait of him *is* lacking in true color and detail. He is what critic Eileen Creelman in the *New York Sun* styled him, "cold . . . unemotional, a puzzle," hardly more than an intellectual exercise. Whether Crowther was also right in his conclusion as to the picture's ultimate stature is another question, one which will continue to be debated. At the moment the voting favors the other side, represented by Howard Barnes' view in the *World-Telegram* that Welles' highly original movie magic had made Kane himself "a full and rich expression of American life . . . a recreation of human experience in human terms rather than a documentary portrait of an individual . . . a dramatization of human experience as only the screen can dramatize it."

John Mosher in the *New Yorker* perhaps put it even better, citing Welles' "elliptical method" by which he simply and clearly "traces a man's life from boyhood to death . . . an involved and specialized character fully depicted."

At last came the San Francisco opening, set for May 14 at RKO's own Golden Gate Theater. But here there would be no formal first night, no glamorous celebrities waving to a mob of adoring fans. In the city nearest to San Simeon and in which Hearst had long been a dominating presence, RKO had grown wary about making any big splash. The picture would start its run quietly at the Golden Gate on the fourteenth, as would any regular feature, its coming announced only by the standard newspaper ads. Then suddenly on May 5 someone or something changed that low-key plan and it was decided to mount a fancy, full-scale opening after all. Preparations for that needed time, so the May 14 opening was abruptly canceled, a fact duly noted by the *San Francisco Chronicle:* "The picture WILL be shown here some day, according to the theater, but not on the 14th, in spite of the elaborate advertising campaign that has been underway for the last week. The postponement was ordered by RKO."

Two weeks of silence followed, then a new date for the opening was announced. In all the city's non-Hearst papers appeared ads declaring that *Citizen Kane* was "Coming to San Francisco!" and would have its festive debut at the Geary Theater on May 27.

Again Welles was on hand, flying in from Los Angeles that morning and taking a room at the Fairmont, where in the afternoon he held court for the press. The *Chronicle* reporter who attended the event filed an account that provides one of the few personal sketches of Welles contemporary with *Kane*'s opening. Its light, bantering tone veils the anonymous writer's obvious admiration for his subject:

> To begin, he entered the room. You will probably not
> see anything meteoric in this unless you happened to
> have been in some room which Mr. Welles has seen

fit to enter. Welles entering a room full of common people is like the sun rising over the backyards of Oakland.

Next, while the room vibrated, he strode to a far corner and seated himself with great violence. Then he leaped up again, seized a rum highball and threw down several draughts. Then the phone rang.

It was Hollywood director Gregory LaCava. Mr. LaCava was being coy and pretending to be somebody Welles didn't know. This buffoonery puzzled and amused the prodigy at first. Then it began to pall on him. Finally it enraged him. Welles roared into the phone, as he alone can roar, and the comic routine on the other end stopped immediately. . . .

He rested one hand on the phone and gazed intently out of the window, which happened to frame a nice picture of the bay. This went on for several minutes, and then Welles turned to look one and all in the eye. He seemed tall, and heavy in the right places, like a fighter. . . . The guests were impressed and sat around waiting for the mercurial maestro to say something. Finally it came. "That was LaCava," he said wanly.

Welles ran a hand through his hair. He moved back to his chair like a ship returning from afar, and settled into it like a parachute out of wind. The guests, expecting something in the nature of another invasion from Mars, waited. Eventually they became restive. Welles was obviously not present in spirit, and would not be unless he were rudely recalled. This is where the press agent came in.

The agent, himself a man of some parts, accomplished the transition from the occult to the actual by the simple process of yelling, "Hey Orson, these people want to ask you some questions." That was all there was to it. Welles came back with a rush and began to talk with grace and a flourish about any and everything.

It came out, suddenly, that Welles had brought his six feet, three-and-one-half-inches of the most vigorous and argumentative flesh to San Francisco to personally grace the opening of the movie, *Citizen Kane.* . . . The agent went on to say that it would open tonight at the Geary Theater, that it was currently sweeping the country, and that it was destined to establish endless precedents in the dramaturgic industry, etc., etc.

Welles, who is too smart to let his ego get anything on him, shaded off the press agent's claims with oral denials accompanied by deprecating gestures, but he didn't fool anybody. The guests, having come fortified with Welles' history and Welles reviews, knew that *Citizen Kane* was indeed all that the press agent said it was.

It was also at the Fairmont that there occurred— shortly after conclusion of the press conference, apparently—the famous accidental meeting in an elevator between the brash Welles and an icy-mannered Hearst. Since the little story was later put into circulation by Welles himself, some have doubted its truth. But at least a portion of it receives support from a contemporary mention in *Variety,* published within six days of the encounter, which places the two men in the same hotel at the same time: "Welles and Hearst both arrived in Frisco the day of the preem, and both stopped at the Fairmont Hotel, a fact which smelled like a Wellesian inspiration, but which proved to be simple coincidence. Its publicity value proved nil, papers here laying off the controversy and killing what seemingly was a press agent's dream." PR man's dream is right. Too bad the papers missed it.

As Welles later described the curious little drama, he was returning to his room from the hotel lobby when he entered an elevator and found himself standing beside the only other passenger. He had to look twice at the man—tall, elderly, well-dressed, with a narrow face and a long, thin nose—before he realized it was Hearst. As the doors shut and the elevator rose, Welles decided that he couldn't let so unlikely, so pregnant a moment pass unobserved.

"Mr. Hearst, my name is Orson Welles," he ventured, his tone friendly and casual. "A movie of mine called *Citizen Kane* is opening tonight here in town. At the Geary Theater over on Mason Street. If you'd care to attend I'd be glad to have some tickets sent to your room. Your personal opinion of the picture I'd find very interesting."

Unmoving, his face a blank, his eyes fixed straight ahead, Hearst ignored the speaker. The elevator stopped, the doors opened and Hearst stepped out. "I'm disappointed in you, Mr. Hearst," Welles couldn't resist calling out as the doors closed, "Kane would have accepted!"

Though it was less brilliant than the Hollywood

opening, with even fewer stars present, the San Francisco premier on the twenty-seventh came off in satisfactory fashion. Welles' arrival at the theater was prolonged and spotlighted—this time not with Dolores Del Rio on his arm but *Kane*'s female lead, Dorothy Commingore. Unlike the previous openings he didn't slip out but stayed until the movie's end, whether or not actually watching it. At the close, as the *Chronicle* told it, he spoke a word to the appreciative, wildly applauding audience.

"Take a bow!" shouted several voices, upon which the audience "refused to be quieted until he walked to the head of the aisle" and offered some remarks. These concerned his nervousness about opening the film in the Hearst stronghold, and his gratification that all had gone so well. "I was afraid you might tear the screen to bits," he is quoted by the *Chronicle,* "but I see now that what we thought was a lot of nerve wasn't."

Reviews in the San Francisco papers (non-Hearst) were all raves, hymning Welles as both director and actor, with a liberal sprinkling of the word "masterpiece." Typical was the *Chronicle*'s notice, written by the same John Hobart who earlier had gone east to report on *Native Son*. Welles' career in show business, he said, resembled nothing so much as "a skyrocket that explodes in successive stages, and his movie debut . . . is the showiest blaze of fireworks he has so far touched off." Hobart even referred—of course without actually naming him, which in San Francisco would have been a cardinal sin—to Hearst and the trouble he'd caused the picture: "Everyone knows how *Citizen Kane* was nearly suppressed because it refers, too specifically it seems, to one powerful and recognizable American contemporary. . . . The important thing is that it has reached the screen."

Interestingly, Hobart discerned in the movie, as its dramatic key, the very same *headlong* quality he'd felt in *Native Son:* "You cannot watch this movie without being swept up in the dramatic tornado that it generates. You are free to despise it or to love it, but there is no avoiding its pummeling force, its sledgehammer melodrama . . . call it theatrical, if you like, but this high-voltage, dynamic theatricality is indeed its unique and wonderful distinction."

❀

It had been a breathless month. Now in a way for Welles the ordeal was over. Delayed though it had been, his complete acceptance as a Hollywood film-maker was an accomplished fact. Still to be suffered through were some anxious moments as all waited to see which way Hearst would jump. Still to be told, also, was the tale of the box office. But no matter what happened with either of those two eventualities, Welles' honored place among Hollywood's best, in his rare fourfold capacity, could no longer be questioned. Late

in June, with the arrival of the July edition of movie-
dom's leading fan magazine, the glossy *Photoplay,* an official cap of sorts was placed on his triumph.

Before this, the popular periodical had pretty well
ignored Welles, conceding him only a brief mention
here or a bare, small photo there, the references never
more than passing. Now in its July 1941 issue it more
than made up for the neglect. Welles it named "The
Man of the Moment," running a full-page portrait of
him alongside a full page of sensitive comment. "The
bitter and doubting reaction of Hollywood" to Welles
pretensions, had been wholly and finally wiped away
by the marvelous success of *Kane.* So impressed was the
Photoplay editor by what he'd seen and heard that he
didn't hesitate to disagree with doubters as to the film's
popular appeal. The public, he assured his readers,
"would go for it in a big way." At the box office as well
as among the critics *Kane* would come out a winner.

All too soon, however, the editor's confident prediction was to prove depressingly wrong, though the real
reason for the financial failure of *Kane* is not the one
usually assigned, the forced shutting down of theaters
led by Hearst. *Kane's* doom, curiously matching the
picture itself, was more complicated than that.

Things had indeed begun well. A week after the
New York opening at the seven-thousand-seat Palace,
Variety reported that it was "the hottest thing in
town. . . . So far it has been within a few bucks of
capacity . . . as the house is scaled on a two-a-day

policy with a $2 top, capacity is $30,800." But within two weeks—*Kane* in the meantime having opened in Chicago and Hollywood—matters had changed drastically, in fact shockingly. Business at New York's Palace, reported *Variety,* had suddenly fallen off (*Kane* was decidedly "not a smash"), and the same was proving true in both Chicago and on the coast.

Already the picture had been pulled from one of the Chicago houses in which it opened, the hope being that sales would improve at the other. It hadn't happened. While the movie business in general in Chicago's Loop, explained *Variety,* had much improved over the previous month, "one exception is *Citizen Kane,* which brodied [took a steep dive] sharply over the weekend and was yanked from the RKO Palace last night after less than a week, with the gross around $7,000. . . . Advance sale was disappointing and the flicker started slowly despite excellent notices." At Hollywood's El Capitan during the same week "receipts were very disappointing." In New York by early June the Palace was down to only 50 percent of capacity.

Everywhere, including Boston and Washington, D.C., where *Kane* debuted late in May, after an initial spurt, ticket sales fell far below expected volume, and gave no sign of recovering.

Long before it played other parts of the country— local theaters in the smaller cities, towns, and villages— long before it felt any impact from the Hearst-inspired lockout by the leading chains, the verdict on *Kane* was in: it would flop, and of its own weight. Those critics who insisted that, despite its obvious merits as art, the picture lacked appeal for a mass audience, that it wouldn't attract viewers seeking a couple hours escape for their money—which meant most people— were right.

As so often, word-of-mouth, the spontaneous judgment of an independent public, had utterly obliterated all the printed superlatives. Now not all the critical praise in the world, heaped up and running over, could save it.

That summer when the picture went into general release, the Hearst-led boycott at last made itself felt, dealing the already staggering film a fatal blow by depriving it of needed outlets. No one has calculated just how many theaters were affected (certainly a thousand or more) nor what percentage of the expected gross the lockout cost. A few of the shut-down houses, to play it safe, paid RKO the usual rental fee, then didn't run the film, depriving the studio of any share in box office receipts.

Any movie would have been derailed by that lethal combination of bad-mouthing and a lockout. But to the fatal equation was added still a third element, to now overlooked, which made total failure inevitable: the looming shadow of war.

By the spring of 1941, when *Kane* opened—some seven months before the attack on Pearl Harbor—fear of being drawn into the European conflict gripped every American home. The topic was inescapable, as front pages and radio stations carried daily reports of the fierce fighting in Europe and heatedly discussed America's possible involvement. As early as May *Variety* reported that "war jitters" had already done serious damage to the entertainment industry as a whole, causing "the recent skid in film house grosses. . . . Uncertainty about the future hurts the box-office more than definite action." Then a week later the paper specifically added: "Managers of theaters, both motion picture and legit, are in a state of complete bewilderment" because ticket sales "have slowed down to a stall. . . . Starting about mid-March grosses began to slide in movie and legit houses, and the slide is today still pronounced and disheartening."

Kane's own shortcomings as entertainment on a popular level, the Hearst boycott, and fear of war—it was that three-pronged handicap, not any single factor, that combined to defeat Orson Welles' ambitious dream of a thundering Hollywood triumph. Showing no profit for the studio, falling far short of recovering its cost (some $150,000 short, it would eventually prove), shunned by distributors and theater managers as box office poison, by year's end *Citizen Kane* was hanging on in only a few isolated theaters across the country.

9

Last Chance

On a shelf in George Schaeffer's Hollywood office sat two gleaming trophies. Awarded by prestigious bodies, the New York Film Critics Circle and the National Board of Review, they honored *Citizen Kane* as Best Picture of 1941. Neither, disappointingly, had sparked any surge of public interest in the movie, at least not at the box office, and now, in February 1942, only a single hope remained: the Academy Awards.

A big splash the night of the awards banquet, and the moribund film might come alive again, at least enough to turn a small profit. Nobody really expected it, but with luck the impossible might happen. Defying all the odds, if it won big it might go through the roof and become a bona fide hit. Stranger things had happened, especially in the volatile world of the movies, and the awards did have that potential.

When the nominations were announced it seemed

that such an exciting outcome might be on the verge of coming true. Leading all contenders, *Kane* garnered no fewer than nine, starting with Best Picture. Welles personally was named in three categories, Best Actor, Best Director, and Best Screenplay (as coauthor with Mankiewicz). There were also nominations for *Kane* in cinematography, sound, art direction, editing, and musical scoring, in all of which Welles had a hand, especially the first two.

Held in the grand ballroom of the Biltmore Hotel in Los Angeles, the awards banquet took place on the night of February 26 with some fifteen hundred people in attendance. The attack on Pearl Harbor having occurred less than three months before, it was the first wartime awards ceremony in Academy history, so a properly sober atmosphere was encouraged. The wearing of formal attire was banned, both men and women being asked to don normal street clothing or military uniforms. A number of female stars, however, showed up in their usual gowned finery, complete with furs and jewelry (Ginger Rogers, Dorothy Lamour, and Linda Darnell were singled out by *Variety* for mention as offenders, "while their sister guests sat around and gnashed their teeth").

On hand was the entire cast of *Kane,* except for Orson Welles. Already he'd begun work on another film—a wartime project, part of a government program meant to raise awareness of U.S. interests in South America—and was on location in Brazil.

To emphasize the serious tone thought proper for

the annual affair, a notable public figure had been invited as guest speaker. This turned out to be Wendell Wilkie, losing opponent to Roosevelt in the 1940 presidential election, a man who had greatly impressed the public and whose opinions were valued. His half-hour speech, delivered after the formal dinner and preceding the awards, called for more aggressive military action in the south pacific against the rampaging Japanese: "We must re-win every foot of soil that has been taken from us . . . we must begin to strike . . . we must begin to win!"

Master of ceremonies for the awards was Bob Hope, and the lesser prizes were handed out first. The winner for art direction (black and white) brought a disappointment, the choice falling on Fox's *How Green Was My Valley*. The editing category followed, and again there was disappointment when the honor went to *Sergeant York*. Also lost to *Kane* were the prizes for sound recording, which went to *That Hamilton Woman,* and musical scoring, won by *The Devil and Daniel Webster.*

The trend away from *Kane* continued with the award for cinematography (black and white), which all viewed as certainly going to Gregg Toland for his revolutionary work on *Kane*. Instead, it went to *How Green Was My Valley*. With Best Original Screenplay *Kane's* slide was halted, the prize going to Welles and Mankiewicz. But then in quick succession, to the great surprise of many in that audience of professionals, the top prizes also slipped out of Welles' grasp.

The award for Best Director had seemed to be Welles' for the taking. It went to John Ford for *How Green Was My Valley.*

Nominated for Best Actor, in addition to Welles, were Cary Grant *(Penny Serenade),* Walter Huston *(The Devil and Daniel Webster),* Gary Cooper *(Sergeant York),* and Robert Montgomery *(Here Comes Mr. Jordan).* Here, possibly, the wartime mood helped determine the choice, for when the envelope was opened Cooper's name was announced as winner. Best Actress went to Joan Fontaine for *Suspicion.*

That left Best Picture, which again almost everyone saw as certainly going to *Kane.* But again the expectations were thwarted: the Oscar went to Ford's *How Green Was My Valley.*

Back then the Academy Awards were not looked on or treated as the entertainment extravaganza they've since become. Newspapers reported the list of winners, with the focus on Best Picture and Best Actor and Actress, without saying much about the affair itself (in 1942 the remarks made by Wilkie were widely quoted, but as a separate story, with only a bare mention that he'd spoken at the awards dinner, and in some cases not even that). An exception was *Variety,* which took the trouble to comment on Welles' stunning defeat, calling it in a headline "The Biggest Upset" in Academy Awards history.

The paper also presumed to identify the reason for the startling outcome, citing the presence in the

Academy voting of a new group, the Hollywood extras. "That most of the 6,000 extras who voted scuttled [Welles'] chances is foregone. The mob prefers a regular guy to a genius." A separate story in that same issue of *Variety* makes the charge more explicit, insisting that Welles was the choice of all true movie-makers:

> The brush given the boy wonder, Orson Welles, is naturally the chief topic of conversation around the gin rummy tables. . . . Into the voting picture, as in other divisions, must be drawn the 6,000 extras, who held the balance of power. These supes must have been influenced, it is generally agreed, by the terrific advertising and publicity campaign given *How Green Was My Valley* by the studio. Also it was a late release and fresher in the minds of the ballot markers.
>
> As for Welles, there is no dissent to the prevailing opinion that the extra vote scuttled him. It was patent that the mob didn't like the guy personally and took it out on him at the polls. The toppers [leading names] among writers, directors, actors, and producers strung along with Welles, as was attested in his nomination in a multiple of brackets, more or less as a direct slap at the way he was treated and maligned by the Hearst papers. Nor did they especially like the way he was sloughed off by the big theater circuits. The strength in numbers overwhelmed him. Maybe it will make him a better guy, or maybe he doesn't give a rap.

The notion that it was the extras vote that deprived Welles of his expected triumph was current at the time and has not so far been challenged. Just why the extras would have gone against him isn't at all clear. In *Kane* he'd used several hundred of them, and there is no record of any difficulty. Welles' biographers, however, for whatever reason, ignore the role played in the 1942 Academy Awards by the extras vote (only one even mentions it, and then in passing). Instead, they offer as a reasonable explanation for Welles' defeat the general feeling against him aroused on his arrival in Hollywood two years before, and supposedly still on the boil.

At the Biltmore on the evening of the awards, says one biographer, "There was a fierce atmosphere against Welles. . . . [He] had carried himself in town like an outsider and a figure of taunting superiority. . . . He had radically outstripped the notions of what kind of film could be made in Hollywood. . . . He needed rebuke, if only because of that monstrous contract."

Another biographer, seemingly on his own authority, claims that the awards audience on that gala night was not coy about expressing resentment of Welles, *why* they would have done so being left vague: "At the first mention of the title, *Citizen Kane,* during the ceremonies, there were eddies of boos, chortles, and hisses throughout the auditorium, in conflict with some dilatory applause. . . . It was a direct humiliation of Welles for causing all the trouble." Surprising as the claim is, especially for that setting and that occasion, no source is cited or suggested (it certainly wasn't the news accounts).

But this is all mere guessing, and in any case it hardly explains the large negative vote among the extras, a bloc-vote, apparently.

One very real possibility, never yet mentioned but which definitely deserves attention, is—once again!—the vengeful hand of William Randolph Hearst. How he might, silently through his well-paid agents, have managed to reach in among the members of the extras guild imposing his will by bribery, or blackmail, or dire threat—his old tried-and-true tactics—doesn't need much imagination to picture. The year 1942, let it be repeated, was the first year in which the extras were given the vote, but in six categories only: Best Picture, Best Song, Best Actor and Actress, and Best Supporting Actor and Actress.

More recent analyses of the 1942 Academy voting pattern have shown that under today's rules, in force since 1957, which restricts voting to Academy members, *Citizen Kane* would have won Best Picture hands down. Welles himself, though facing strong competition from Gary Cooper's timely soldier role, might have captured the Best Actor award. Best Director would also have been his.

Full proof of Hearst's part in the ultimate defeat of Orson Welles is likely beyond retrieving. But where a man of Hearst's savage reputation is concerned, where no despicable or vindictive act is out of bounds or beyond the reach of money, in some things for some minds it isn't needed.

As much as anyone, Hearst was aware that a Welles triumph that night might well have resurrected, and certainly would have given final approval to, the hated film.

But fixing the Academy Awards, if in fact he did so, was not Hearst's last, vengeful swipe at *Citizen Kane*. That came a year later when the hapless Herman Mankiewicz handed him an opening that brought rushing to the fore all his ugly old killer instinct. Incredibly, the incident that triggered it, involving a drunk-driving charge against Mankiewicz, actually took place at Hearst's front door.

Though she spent most of her time at San Simeon, Marion Davies had always insisted on having a separate place of her own, bought for her by Hearst. For long it was a magnificent home on the beach at Santa Monica. By March 1943 it was an equally magnificent Mediterranean villa in Beverly Hills (in fact, the house in which eight years later Hearst would die). By strange coincidence, this house was situated barely a mile from Mankiewicz's own Beverly Hills home on Tower Road.

On the evening of March 11, 1943, Mankiewicz left work at Universal, stopped off at Romanoff's for several drinks—or more than several—then drove himself home. Cutting through Benedict Canyon, at a spot on North Beverly Drive he carelessly allowed his car to drift over the center line into the path of an oncoming vehicle, a small station wagon. The collision was almost head-on, the nose of Mankiewicz's car smashing into the swerving station wagon's left front fender. Both drivers had managed to brake somewhat, so the resulting impact was not so devastating as it might have been. A witness phoned the police, who arrived within minutes.

In the other car were three women. One of them, the driver, was the wife of Ira Gershwin, George's brother. With her was her husband's secretary, and her laundress (the Gershwins' home was also in the vicinity). No one was hurt badly, though Mrs. Gershwin sustained a gash on her forehead, on the right side near the temple, as well as bruised knees. The other women, while considerably shaken, were unharmed. Mankiewicz also escaped injury.

Mrs. Gershwin was taken to a Beverly Hills hospital where the cut on her forehead was closed with three stitches, and she was sent home. Mankiewicz, obviously under the influence, was taken to the Beverly Hills police station where he was booked. Five hours later he was released on $500 bail.

As it happened, Hearst himself was at the time staying at the Davies house. Someone from the house went out to check on the noise of the crash, and Hearst was soon informed of Mankiewicz's identity. The next morning's *Los Angeles Examiner*, a Hearst paper, headlined a story on page three: "Mrs. Gershwin Hurt; Film Writer Arrested." The story also went out on the Hearst wire (International News Service), and for the next week Hearst papers across the country carried daily page-one stories on the accident. In all of them Mankiewicz's name was prominent and every slightest detail of the accident and subsequent events was highlighted. Mrs. Gershwin's cut forehead and bruised knees at first were not specified, only the fact that, along with "two others," she had been "injured."

On March 14 Hearst's New York tabloid, the *Mirror,* headlined, "Hold Writer In Hollywood Car Collision." The story said that Mankiewicz "admitted that he had been drinking," but later after being booked at the police station had "created such a disturbance in his cell it was necessary to remove his shoes." That same day the Hearst paper in Milwaukee, the *Sentinel,* carried this page-one story:

SCREEN WRITER FACES
DRUNK TRIAL MONDAY

Felony Complaint Will Be Asked in Case of Herman Mankiewicz

Los Angeles, March 13—Herman Mankiewicz, 45, scenarist, is scheduled to answer to a drunk driving charge at 2 p.m. Monday in the courtroom of Beverly Hills Police Judge Charles Griffin.

The charge arose from an automobile crash Thursday evening in Beverly Hills in which Mrs. Lenora Gershwin, wife of Ira Gershwin, the composer, and two others were injured.

While the writer remained at liberty on $500 bail, posted after he spent five hours in jail, Beverly Hills Police Chief C.H. Anderson said a felony complaint would be sought against Mankiewicz from Beverly Hills City Atty. Richard Waitz.

"All indications," said the police chief, "are that personal injuries are involved," and for that reason, he added, the felony complaint against the writer is to be sought. . . .

Later at the police station where he reportedly failed to pass sobriety tests given by Police Sgt. P. R. Smith and Police Surgeon Ralph Lewis, the writer, police said, stated: "I am drunk. I know I am drunk. Let's get this over with." And when he was jailed, he began vigorously to protest his imprisonment, saying, the police added, "I am Mr. Mankiewicz. I have no right to be here. This is an injustice. I want out of here."

His statements were emphasized by such kicking against the cell, said police, that it was necessary for them to remove his shoes to end the disturbance. On their report police made a notation that Mankiewicz was "insulting, sarcastic, impolite, and talkative."

Pending x-rays which her husband said were to be taken, the full extent of Mrs. Gershwin's injuries were not known. She was first treated at the Beverly Hills receiving hospital for a deep gash over the right temple and bruised knees, and then removed to her home.

The remainder of the lengthy account quotes the arresting officer on the scene as saying that when he had Mankiewicz walk across the street as a test of sobriety, "he stumbled and nearly fell. His gait was staggering, his speech was slurred, and he was quite talkative. His eyes and pupils were dilated." The Hearst reporter also checked the Beverly Hills police records and found that a dozen years before, in 1931, Mankiewicz had been ticketed, as the story carefully pointed out, for "allegedly failing to make a boulevard stop," but the case had been dismissed.

The continuation of the story on page two—the whole story occupies a surprising twenty-five column inches, more than most that day including the war reportage—also carries a two-tiered headline. "Screen Writer Injures Three," it inaccurately stated in large type. A subhead in smaller type declares, "Felony Charge May Add to Mankiewicz Troubles."

Next day the pounding continued. "Drunk Driving Hearing Today for Scenarist," announced the *Sentinel's* page-one story, adding that "new and important witnesses" were being subpoenaed to testify at the pending trial. The names of these new witnesses, though, "the Chief declined to divulge . . . in advance of a formal hearing." If Mankiewicz did go to trial, and was convicted, the paper said, his punishment would be severe: "The charge on which the well-to-do motion picture writer is now at freedom on $500 bail, carries the maximum punishment, if he is convicted, of one to ten years imprisonment."

The story concludes with the Beverly Hills police chief vowing to safeguard "the streets of this community

against intoxicated and reckless drivers. The Mankiewicz case seems like a flagrant one, and we are determined that it shall be justly handled."

Through all of this, no non-Hearst paper of promi-
nence picked up the story, not one. Then at last both
Time and *Newsweek* took note of it, but only to jeer. In
its issue for March 29, *Newsweek* recapped the bare
facts, commenting that after the *Examiner*'s initial story,

> other members of the [Hearst] chain across the coun-
> try did likewise, complete with stories and pictures,
> including a photodiagram of an interlocked coupe
> and station wagon on the palm-lined Benedict Can-
> yon Road.
>
> Ever alert to screen credits, Hollywood remem-
> bered immediately that Mankiewicz had collabo-
> rated with Orson Welles on the screenplay of "Citi-
> zen Kane," which spun the life of a publisher in
> none-too-flattering terms, and ever since has drawn
> the wrath of the Hearst press.

Unexpectedly, that ended Hearst's interest in Mankiewicz and his accident. In May the case went to trial
(very probably under some personal, behind-the-scenes
prodding by Hearst demanding protection, as he
would have disguised his purpose, for the Beverly Hills
community). Only by means of a hung jury did Mankiewicz escape conviction and a stiff jail sentence.

His screenwriting career, however, was virtually
ended. Over the next ten years, until his death in April

1953 from liver damage, he managed to find work on only four more pictures. Three of them were for RKO.

❀

In different degrees other members of the *Kane* company felt Hearst's vengeful hand. In her 1980 biography, Ruth Warrick, who played the first Mrs. Kane, claimed that her career was hampered by Hearst's ability to limit and even deny her the necessary publicity. "Like all the cast," she wrote, "I remained a non-person in the Hearst press for several years." Somehow she managed to survive, "and even flourish during my exile from the powerful Hearst press. But there was no doubt that being pariahs made good parts elusive for most of the *Kane* cast." Among other things, she explained, her name would be deleted by Hearst editors from any ads or publicity they ran on her movies, even when a studio other than RKO was concerned. (Eventually Warrick built up a satisfying film career, at last gaining great popularity on television for her role as Phoebe Tyler in the long-running soap opera *All My Children*.)

A potentially more serious instance of Hearst's vengeance on a *Kane* cast member concerns Dorothy Commingore, who so well filled the Marion Davies role—of course thereby making herself a special target of Hearst's ire. No actual evidence exists to link him with what happened to Commingore, so that even a mention of the possibility must smack uncomfortably of Hearst's own methods. Yet putting certain facts on record, considering all the circumstances, seems justified. More precise information will surface some day either to confirm or deny his responsibility.

After *Kane,* for which she received high praise from the critics—in fact second only to Welles himself— RKO saw that it had a new star on its hands. Typical of much that was written about her was this column from *Cue* magazine:

> Dorothy Commingore, green-eyed, red-headed and 21, has hoisted herself from obscurity to the cinematic heights by way of a single role. As the blond second spouse in awesome Orson Welles' *Citizen Kane,* her intensely realistic portrayal of the 40-year span in a woman's life—from shopgirl to tycoon's wife to boozy hag—has won her a long-term contract with RKO. Miss Commingore's wide range of dramatic talents are to be allowed full play in forthcoming feature roles (first in a "sophisticated" comedy, then a western) and there's talk—serious this time—of grooming her to outshine Bette Davis.
>
> The brief career of this new shooting star has been consistently unconventional . . . Urged by a visiting stock company to try acting, Miss Commingore became an artist's model, then joined the Carmel (Cal.) Summer Stock Theatre. There, she was

Right: A rave review in *Cue* magazine (July 1941) for Dorothy Commingore's performance in *Kane,* predicting a rivalry with Bette Davis.

SUCCESS STORY

Dorothy Comingore, green-eyed red-headed, and 21, has hoisted herself from obscurity to the cinematic heights by way of a single rôle. As the blonde second spouse in awesome Orson Welles' *Citizen Kane*, her intensely realistic portrayal of the 40-year span in a woman's life—from shopgirl to tycoon's wife to boozy hag —has won her a long-term contract with RKO. Miss Comingore's wide range of dramatic talents are to be allowed full play in forthcoming featured rôles (first in a "sophisticated" comedy. then a Western) and there's talk—serious this time—of grooming her to outshine Bette Davis.

The brief career of this new shoot-

discovered by none other than Charles Chaplin, at his suggestion was signed by Warners for a 3-months' trial, and was as promptly forgotten. A discouraging procession of extra and bit parts in the movies followed, until Welles, in quest of *Citizen Kane*'s feminine lead, met Commingore at a Hollywood cocktail party. . . . Critics and directors have thrown her kudos for her "uncanny sense of timing." Up-and-coming Commingore has indubitably come to the cinema to stay.

Cue's prediction of a brilliant future for the young actress was echoed by reviews generally, but as the subsequent decade would prove, all were wrong, sadly and strangely wrong.

Soon after the debut of *Kane*, RKO cast her in the lead in a comedy, *Unexpected Uncle*. Something happened, however, something never explained, and she was dropped from the picture, to be replaced by Anne Shirley. Next it was announced that she would star in a western, *Valley of the Sun*, but there was another sudden and unexplained change. Again she was dropped and her role given to another, this time Lucille Ball. Three full years then went by in which, though still under contract to RKO, the studio found no work for her. When she did again fill a role, it was not for RKO but with an independent production, a supporting role in Eugene O'Neil's *The Hairy Ape*, starring Susan Hayward. Her efforts won praise, if from a slightly negative angle, from the *New York Times:* "Unfortunately,

Dorothy Commingore as the patient foil has a role offering her little opportunity for her proven acting talent."

No less than five years passed before her next outing, and it was only a bit part in a Clark Gable film of 1949, *Any Number Can Play* (MGM). Two years after that she appeared in another independent production, which proved to be her last movie: *The Big Night,* with John Barrymore Jr. and Preston Foster. With that she dropped from sight, and except for one shocking episode wasn't heard of again until her death in 1971.

In 1953, according to the news accounts, she was arrested in Hollywood on a charge of soliciting for purposes of prostitution. The charge, however, was dropped and she was sent to a psychiatric ward of Los Angeles County Hospital as an alcoholic. About that startling development a little more appears in Ruth Warrick's 1980 memoir. After Commingore's divorce in 1950, writes Warrick, "she began to drink heavily, sitting in Musso-Frank's and bending any available ear with her tale of injustice," the nature of the "tale" left unspecified. The photographs of her in the news accounts of the arrest, adds Warrick, "with the harsh flashbulbs revealing the marks of her life, looked eerily like the face of Susan Alexander Kane as seen in the final scene of the film."

The photograph she mentions is probably the one that appeared with the *New York Post* story on March 20, 1953. Full-face, it shows her with features pinched and drawn, and with her hair pulled back tight under a floppy, unflattering hat.

During this same period, 1952–53, she was among the many screen actors called by Congress to testify before the House Un-American Activities Committee, regarding alleged communist ties. She appeared, declared herself to be a loyal American, and demanded to know who had accused her, then refused to answer any questions. No further action was reported.

Her refusal to testify before the House also came up in the context of her arrest on the prostitution charge. The arrest, she asserted, was a "frame-up," caused by her silence before the committee in Washington. "I've had nothing but trouble lately," she is quoted as explaining in the *San Francisco Chronicle*. "My phone has been tapped and my house ransacked. I guess I shouldn't have been an unfriendly witness." Who might have done the ransacking and the tapping she doesn't say.

Neither are the circumstances of the arrest, which occurred in Hollywood, quite clear. The *New York Post* version (not taken from a wire service but labeled "Special to the *New York Post*"), is told in four brief sentences:

> Deputy Sheriffs William Baker and Peter Escanilla, on their nightly anti–vice patrol, said they picked her up in a car last night and bought her a few drinks. "Let's go to a dark place," they quoted her as saying.
>
> They drove to a spot near Plummer Park, said the deputies, and Baker asked, "How much?" Baker said he gave her a marked bill, and then made the arrest.

Ex-Movie Star Held as Prostitute

Special to the New York Post 1953

Hollywood, March 19—Red-haired Dorothy Comingore, 40, one of filmland's most glamorous actresses when she starred opposite Orson Welles in "Citizen Kane" 13 years ago, was under arrest today as a prostitute.

The former glamor girl, who lost custody of her two children last November after her ex-husband charged her with excessive drinking and Communist affiliations, awaited a Municipal Court hearing in the county jail for lack of $500 bail.

Deputy Sheriffs William Baker and Pete Escanilla, on their nightly anti-vice patrol, said they picked her up in a car last night and bought her a few drinks.

"Let's go to a dark place," they quoted her as saying.

They drove to a spot near Plummer Park, said the deputies, and Baker asked: "How much?"

Charges Frame-Up

Baker said he gave her a marked bill and then made the arrest. Miss Comingore, whose name once was linked romantically with Charlie Chaplin, charged the arrest was a "frame-up" caused by her refusal last fall to testify before the House Un-American Activities Committee in its hunt for Hollywood Communists.

"I've had nothing but trouble lately," she said. "My phone has been tapped and my house ransacked. I guess I shouldn't have been an unfriendly witness."

The actress divorced screen writer Richard Collins in 1946 and later married magazine editor Theodore Strauss, whom she divorced shortly afterward. She and Collins waged a bitter court battle over custody of their two

DOROTHY COMINGORE

children, Judith, 11, and Michael, 8.

In 1951 Collins, an admitted ex-Communist, gave the House committee the names of 25 movie people who he said were members of the Communist Party.

Her last film was "The Hairy Ape," with William Bendix.

Dorothy Commingore's 1953 arrest, a dozen years after starring as Mrs. Kane, was widely reported. This story appeared in the *New York Post*, March 20, 1953.

That same day the story also went out on the United Press wire and it was picked up by the *San Francisco Chronicle*. In this version Commingore claims that she was the victim of a plain old-fashioned police hustle:

> Miss Commingore was arrested by Sheriff's vice squad officers who said she approached them in a Hollywood bar and suggested that they drive "to some dark place." They accepted her offer, and revealed their identity after she allegedly demanded $10 for her love.
>
> The green-eyed actress, who gained her fame in Orson Welles' "Citizen Kane," had a different story. She said the officers offered to drive her home after buying her a drink, and took her to jail instead.

Trial was set for April 10, but the charge was dropped when Commingore agreed to seek treatment as an alcoholic.

She died, at age fifty-eight, on December 30, 1971, in Lawrence Memorial Hospital, New London, Connecticut. Local papers identified her as Mrs. Dorothy Crowe of Lord's Point, Stonington, Connecticut. The cause of death is given only as a "longtime illness." (There had been two previous marriages, both with Hollywood connections, both ending in divorce. She had two children born of her first marriage, Judith, born shortly after the filming of *Kane,* and Michael, born 1945.)

Whether Hearst had any link to the sad chronicle of Dorothy Commingore's fall cannot at the moment be said. Given his known ruthlessness in his journalistic pursuits, however, and his savage way of exacting revenge, that possibility cannot be brushed aside. Wrecking her film career by exerting pressure in the industry to deny her roles, or good roles, was certainly within his power, perhaps more so because of a tendency among studio heads to compensate for the release of *Kane,* making up for their failure to stop the movie. Accusations of communist leanings were, of course, with Hearst a favorite method of attack. In the atmosphere of the time such charges were all too easy to level.

❀

A gaunt, physically wasted figure, William Randolph Hearst lay stretched at full length on a bed. At 125 pounds he was less than half his normal weight. His already long, narrow face was painfully thinned, suggesting emaciation, the skin pulled tight over forehead and cheeks. He was in an upstairs bedroom of the sumptuous and secluded Beverly Hills home of his mistress, the Mediterranean villa behind high hedges at 1007 North Beverly Drive.

Now aged eighty-eight, suffering from a heart condition made worse by the complications of old age, his death is expected at any moment. It is mid-August 1951.

In the house, waiting for the inevitable, are two of his five sons, as well as an assortment of relatives and friends with their children, along with nurses, doctors, secretaries, and servants. Also on hand is Marion

Davies, walking a sharp edge of nervousness and steadily drinking to calm herself. ("Drinking neat scotch," her biographer frankly states, "in quantities that suggested she was really hoping for unconsciousness.") In the early hours of the morning of August 14, urged by the doctor to rest, she went up to bed. Given a sedative by injection, she was soon sound asleep.

Not until noontime did she awaken, and then on getting up she was informed that Hearst was dead. The attending nurse had left him alone for a moment just before ten. Returning, she found him without a pulse and not breathing. When the distraught Marion said she wanted to see the body she was told she couldn't. It was no longer in the house. It had already been taken away by hearse.

"I asked where he was," she was quoted as saying later, "and the nurse said he was dead. His body was gone, whoosh, like that. Old W. R. was gone. The boys were gone. I was alone."

From that moment, so far as the Hearst family could control it, Marion Davies was blotted out of the dead man's life. When mentioned at all in the news accounts she is first identified as the star of his movies, then, almost as an afterthought, as "his friend and confidante." The house in which he died was identified as his own, "his Beverly Hills mansion." (Later a few papers revealed the fact that, according to county records, the Beverly Hills house was actually "the property of the former actress.")

Everywhere newspapers noted Hearst's passing, most offering lengthy obituary articles supplied by the different wire services in which were laid out his whole life and career. Not surprisingly, there was much outright praise for the dead tycoon from prominent people, especially those who in one way or another had come within the orbit of his money or influence, or who had known him only in his more conservative latter days. These included a wide selection of public figures, such as General Douglas McArthur (Hearst had boomed him for president), General Omar Bradley, Bernard Baruch, former president Herbert Hoover, and New York's Cardinal Spellman. All these, it seems, thought Hearst a "great" man, at least were willing to be quoted as saying so.

Many others withheld judgment, saying that it would be foolish, just then, to attempt a final appraisal of so influential a sixty-year career. All did grant, however, that Hearst would be "alternately praised and damned, his achievements drawing maledictions here and hosannas there." Only a few commentators, the more realistic among journalists—those not overly dazzled by Hearst's sheer ability to build circulation, never mind how—said outright what all were thinking: "He brought shock and bitter outrage to the respectable, as the cool, unscrupulous, and brilliantly inventive exponent of 'yellow' journalism. He wanted to sell papers and he did, spending money like water to buy the ablest brains he could enlist, driving them to every kind of 'stunt' and sensational exploit. . . . A new form of journalism, it horrified many by its tendency toward irresponsibility and vulgarism."

All the Hearst papers, of course, took the opposite tack, unabashedly calling their departed Chief "the greatest figure in American journalism, whose patriotism and wisdom had been a strongly guiding influence in the nation." (That was the lead in the *San Francisco Herald-Examiner*'s page-one story on August 15, the paper's second edition that same day. It had been improved from the original lead in the first edition, which claimed more sedately that Hearst's career as a publisher had "ushered in the modern era of American journalism.)

It was an editorial in the *Nation* that most courageously and ably speared what it called the "adulation" of the dead man then being quoted from so many eminent personages. For the amoral, unscrupulous Hearst,

> it was merely a question of paying more than anybody else for anyone or anything he wanted. . . . Wherever originality was required or money was not sufficient, Hearst failed. . . . Though his own private life was far from straight-laced, he did not hesitate to ruin, for purposes of circulation the private lives of those who could not retaliate. In many ways Hearst was the poor little rich boy of "Citizen Kane." He asked for a newspaper as some children might ask for a peppermint stick. . . .
>
> Have American values become so distorted that

a gargoyle can be mistaken for the image of a saint? That Hearst should be honored as a public figure in public statements by high government officials and leaders from all walks of life is most disturbing evidence of the idolatry of sheer wealth and power and magnitude which seems to obsess so many Americans.

The unctuous eulogy of Mayor Impelliterri of New York only emphasizes the degrading spectacle of the American flag being flown at half-mast on the City Hall out of respect to the memory of a man of whose public accomplishments it would be better to say nothing.

But perhaps the most curious, most puzzling thing of all about Hearst's passing is the fact that in all the many newspaper obituary articles looked at for this study, except for that one slight mention in the *Nation,* the link with *Citizen Kane* is completely ignored. Even as his many undeniable errors and excesses are candidly detailed, his multitude of failings and misadventures, no writer pauses to recall the bitter battle over the movie that had so starkly summed up those faults. It is true that there had intervened nine years and one terrible war, and *Kane* had not since been shown in public. Yet those reasons are hardly sufficient in themselves to explain so glaring an oversight. Nor does the old apprehension over libel suits or other legal action, previously intimidating fears that ended with Hearst's passing, account for the curious silence.

But what does?

❀

During the ten years that Hearst lived after the *Citizen Kane* affair, no evidence shows him as continuing to harass or target Welles. Nor has anyone yet thought to suggest, even offhandedly, any such sustained vendetta. In that last decade of Hearst's life the struggling Welles managed to complete five more pictures *(Ambersons, Journey into Fear, The Stranger, Lady from Shanghai, Macbeth)*. But that was less than half of what he might have expected to do, and all were plagued with difficulties of production, financing, and control. Only one of the five made a little money *(The Stranger)*.

Whether those ten troublesome, less than triumphant years were solely a result of Welles' own shortcomings, or of sheer bad luck, or might have been to some extent a result of Hearst's secret manipulation, must for now remain an open question.

The presently prevailing notion, assumed by all, that with *Kane* on the shelf and moribund after 1942, Hearst dismissed all thought of the young man who had so gallingly upset his life, is not really convincing. If someday evidence should surface to show that while he lived Hearst went on quietly hounding the youthful genius—threatening those who would employ him, blocking his access to needed funding—no one who knows him will be the least surprised.

10

Then Is Heard No More

At the front door of a small, plain two-story house near Laurel Canyon in the Hollywood Hills stands a young man, his finger pressing the bell. It is ten o'clock on the morning of October 10, 1985, a sunny morning promising another fair day.

The young man's name is Fred Gillet. He is chauffeur and personal assistant to the seventy-year-old Orson Welles. The small house, rented by Welles on a monthly basis, is a second home. In Las Vegas, two hundred miles away, he has another house which he owns and where he stays when he's not in Los Angeles. There lives his wife of thirty years, Paola, with their daughter Beatrice, twenty-eight. His other daughters, born of his first two wives, Virginia Nicholson and Rita Hayworth, are on their own.

After several rings of the bell without an answer, Gillet pushes open the unlocked door and enters the house. Mr. Welles has an appointment that morning for which he must on no account be late.

The night before, Gillet had driven him home from Ma Maison Restaurant, where he often ate supper, sometimes with friends, more often alone. Last night he'd been with friends, including his latest biographer, Barbara Leaming. Her book, on which Welles collaborated, had been published barely three weeks before. That afternoon the two had taped a segment of a talk show plugging the book (Merv Griffin).

Calling out "Mr. Welles?" Gillet went from room to room on the first floor, getting no response. Probably still in bed, he thought, starting up the stairs. When a knock on the bedroom door brought no response, the chauffeur pushed it softly open, and was startled to see his employer slumped in an easy chair near the bed.

No longer the handsome, dark-haired, vibrant figure he'd once been, but a bloated graybeard weighing almost three hundred pounds, Welles was enveloped in a loose-fitting bathrobe. His head was thrown grotesquely to one side, resting on the chairback. Before him was a small table on which sat a typewriter holding a sheet of paper. His eyes were closed.

Hurrying over, the young chauffeur again anxiously murmured, "Mr. Welles?" There was no response, no movement. Gently he touched the massive arm, getting no reaction. Nor did Welles appear to be breathing.

Then, even while fearing he was too late—he knew about Welles' heart condition, having driven him to the doctor for a checkup only the week before—he dialed a paramedic number. Uncertain what to do next, he finally turned and left the room, going downstairs to wait at the open front door.

Within five minutes a police car pulled up at the house and two officers went up to the bedroom. Their examination took only a few seconds. Welles was dead.

Everywhere the news earned front-page attention, beginning that same afternoon when the *Los Angeles Times* headlined, "ORSON WELLES FOUND DEAD AT HOME." In most papers over the next few days appeared lengthy obituary articles detailing his entire career, the smaller papers reprinting pieces from the larger dailies and the wire services. All reported that he was alone when, at some unknown moment in the thirteen hours since he was last seen, he died. All stressed the verdict that his death was from "natural causes," with heart attack eventually specified.

Prominent in the obituaries was mention of *Citizen Kane* as his undoubted masterpiece, and its having been voted on several authoritative lists the greatest film of all. But in only a few reports was the great film's troubled link with Hearst noted, and then only in passing. None gave any real sense of the old ugly battle, then four decades in the past.

Also prominently noted was another large part of the Welles legend, his sad failure to reach the top again in the long stretch of years since *Kane,* his having in the end fallen short of true, sustained greatness. Some commentators, a very few, disagreeing with that assessment, cited his work on other films through the years (*Magnificent Ambersons* in 1942, *Touch of Evil* in 1958, *Chimes at Midnight* in 1966). But most went along with the widespread feeling that, as one leading paper expressed it, his career after *Kane* "was one of largely unfulfilled promise." Though he was certainly a genius, said another paper using nearly the same words, "his talents remained unfulfilled."

Possible explanations for the breakdown of such great abilities, the waste and dissipation of Welles notable artistic drive, were readily attempted in his obituaries. "He became virtually unemployable because of his inability to finish projects," was the suggestion of the *Los Angeles Times,* laying the cause to psychological flaws. Rather more specific was the *Chicago Tribune,* and more practical. Welles' career, it stated with assurance, had been "cut short through a combination of his bucking authority and, perhaps, through [his own] self-destructive impulses. . . . Controversy and clashes with studio executives dogged his every move."

Foreshadowing the two sides of the debate which still today reverberates in books and articles, was the comment supplied in one brief paragraph by the *New York Times* on the day after Welles' passing: "For his failure to realize his dreams Welles blamed his critics and the financiers of Hollywood. Others blamed what they described as his erratic, egotistical, self-indulgent, and self-destructive temperament. . . . Loud, brash, amusing and insufferable by turns, he made friends and enemies by the score."

No doubt there is some truth in all of those comments. What no one then or since has bothered dwelling on is the fact that Welles at a very early age had already absorbed the dangerous knowledge that in whatever he did he could get away with pleasing himself alone. Beginning when he was five, as an authentic child prodigy rather amazing in his knowledge and abilities—all of them recognized and recorded at the time—he was endlessly pampered and indulged by those around him. Almost inevitable was the peremptory, self-gratifying personality that resulted, not hidden but out in the open for all to see, as his biographers have candidly reported.

In a fundamental way Welles' life and career are explained by what he learned as a child. *Citizen Kane* was a triumph because, having exacted from RKO an extraordinary degree of control over his first film, he made it to please himself. His startling success didn't last because that unprecedented control didn't last, and he'd never learned the necessity—in movie-making above all—of sometimes pleasing others.

A question asked in the *Newsweek* obituary piece makes exactly that point in different words: "Why couldn't Welles hang on and increase that power, that leadership that blazed so astonishingly? . . . Perhaps the precocity went sour before it became maturity. . . . His carnivorous appetite for art was gradually diluted by other appetites." *The precocity went sour*—that, sadly, is very often what happens to prodigies, especially those unlucky enough to be born with a variety of large appetites and who never learn to curb them.

Another revealing remark about Welles, warmer and more human and thus going deeper—a sort of puzzled shake of the head hinting at forces beyond knowing—was offered by a man who in his youth had worked closely with Welles on *Citizen Kane*. Robert Wise, later a highly respected director, as a twenty-five-year-old had the heady experience of being chosen by Welles himself to do the principal editing on *Kane*. Asked after Welles' death to comment on his old boss he responded, more thoughtfully than at first may appear: "Orson Welles was, I think, as close to a genius as anyone I ever met. Dynamic, creative, full of life, loved stories, loved food, loved ladies. It's kind of sad but looking back on it, *Citizen Kane* seems sort of autobiographical—Kane, big talent, big career, downhill, downhill, losing it all in the end."

Whether a final word or words fell from Welles' lips in those last moments alone in his Hollywood home, some whispered word of despair or regret, none will ever know. If any did, it can be taken as certain that no fond memories were called up by such utterance of happy boyhood days, in the snow or otherwise. The Welles boyhood had been passed in Kenosha, Wisconsin, where he was born and where his family had lived and prospered since before the Civil War. During his life he had let it be known on several occasions that his view of little Kenosha was decidedly *not* of the nostalgic Rosebud variety. A life begun in an obscure backwater town fifty miles north of Chicago was not something he liked to acknowledge, and in later years he often tried to give himself a more exotic origin. His dour feelings about his Wisconsin beginnings were well-known, and in the lengthy obituary account that appeared in Kenosha's hometown paper, the *Kenosha News,* on October 11, 1985, that knowledge found wry expression, starting with the headline:

HIS KIND OF TOWN, KENOSHA WASN'T

By Don Jensen, Staff Writer

Orson Welles once referred to Kenosha as the "nasty little town" where he was born. Usually, though, he ignored us, preferring to tell biographers that he was conceived in Paris or Rio while his parents were on a global junket.

With that sort of spit-in-the-eye attitude toward the old hometown, it's understandable if Kenoshans are more than willing to disinherit our prodigal son who died Thursday in Los Angeles at age 70.

Surely Welles would never qualify for a Chamber

of Commerce booster medal. But he was a true genius, a monumental, multi-faceted genius, a polished gem, and a sly rogue, a genuine original. And even though he may have rejected us, he was and will remain in memory.

Sorry, Orson, wherever you are, like it or not, you are a Kenoshan. And if it makes the rest of you feel any better, know this—Orson was a first-class bullshooter! So maybe we can convince ourselves that he really didn't mean all those nasty things he said about us.

But of course he did mean them, fiercely and wholeheartedly meant them, not about Kenosha itself, its ordinary neighbors and quiet streets, but about what had happened to him there. Better than anyone he knew where and when it was that he learned the fatal trick of always pleasing himself, getting his own way in everything, that lifelong quirk of temperament which lifted him to the heights, and then slowly yet surely destroyed him.

Between Kane and Welles, it would seem, there really is a certain curious similarity.

As he lay dying, Kane saw how his grotesquely distorted life was the inevitable result of his own deliberate choices, not of any deprivation of love in his boyhood. That's what Rosebud meant for Kane, his own culpability in the loss of his soul, even as he gained the whole world.

Welles, in his last hours alone in his Hollywood home, may have remembered playing that climactic scene from his great movie, may have recalled the burning moment when that final poignant word fell from his lips. Perhaps he too faced the truth at last, that the blame for his own sadly distorted life lay not with his upbringing but, as in the end it does with all men, with himself.

Yet there was, as Welles himself belatedly confessed, a Rosebud of sorts in his past which did in a curious way color his boyhood. Where Kane's Rosebud concerned a simple boy's sled in the snow, Welles' related more dramatically to some secret visits he paid when a boy to a ghostly dance hall in another town.

During the 1920s his father owned a small hotel in a town in northern Illinois called Grand Detour, some hundred miles southwest of Kenosha. Beginning at six or seven he spent time there every year, until in 1928 when he was twelve a fire destroyed the building. Interviewed a year or two before his death, he recalled Grand Detour as "a marvelous little corner in time . . . a kind of forgotten place . . . where I do see some kind of Rosebud." His youthful days there, he recalled, had been, "a completely anachronistic, old-fashioned, early-Tarkington, rural kind of life, with a country store that had above it a ballroom with an old dance floor with springs in it, so that folks would feel light on their feet. When I was little nobody had danced up there for many years. But I used to sneak up at night and dance by moonlight with the dust rising from the floor."

That deserted chamber, it may be, with its strangely unstable floor and clouds of dust floating pale in the moonlight, held for the aging prodigy the aching memory of all he'd once dreamed, all that might have been.

Appendix A:
Citizen Kane in Film History

Appendix B:
Citizen Kane in Hearst Biography

Notes and Sources

Selected Bibliography

Index

Appendix A
Citizen Kane *in Film History*

For Orson Welles, the decades-long descent from the heights held at least one saving touch of grace. Beginning in 1962, most of the world saw him as the creator—not to mention *star*—of the greatest movie ever made.

In that year *Citizen Kane* first appeared at the very top of the most prestigious list of all-time greatest movies, placed in its number one spot by a vote of the critics (survey by *Sight and Sound,* official magazine of the British Film Institute). Similar votes taken by *Sight and Sound* in 1972 and 1982 repeated that signal triumph, so for his last twenty or so years Welles enjoyed a professional distinction unknown by any other filmmaker, ever. True, there would have been times when that distinction, enforcing the cruel contrast with his later aimless meandering, was more of a burden than an honor. Life does that, sometimes, especially to those in its higher reaches, giving with one hand while taking with the other. Like most people, though—those who are past the age of thirty, say, and who've been around some—Welles was able to take it all pretty much as it came.

His wait for the top ranking had not been unduly drawn out, since for half of those twenty years *Kane* had reposed unseen in RKO's vaults. Only in the mid-fifties did it again appear in movie houses, and begin filtering back into public consciousness. Along with this increased viewing came steadily widening written discussion—in books and articles—here and in Europe, France in particular. No longer hampered and roiled by the Hearst connection, professional film commentators revealed new depths of insight in the picture, or made plain what had been hidden. As with great works of literature, abstruse or invisible meanings were turned up, of a sort never consciously intended by the author/creator, but valid and fascinating once seen.

In no time, the body of critical discussion about *Kane* equaled, then exceeded that for any other film.

Kane's first mention in the list of great films came in 1952, but only as a runner-up to the top ten (*The Bicycle Thief* headed that list). In 1962 *Kane* leaped all the way to the top spot (*The Bicycle Thief* dropping to a tie for sixth and only two others of the 1952 list surviving).

In 1972 *Kane* held firm at number one, while the other nine from 1962 were juggled around or dropped. *The Bicycle Thief* disappeared from the list altogether.

In this same round-up, quite unexpectedly, the second movie Welles made for RKO, *The Magnificent Ambersons* (1942), earned a tie for number eight (*Ambersons* is another story, beyond the scope of the present pages).

The list for 1982, again with ten choices, was again headed by *Kane*. Only four others from the 1972 list survived, *Ambersons* being one. Making all four lists was only a single title, Eisenstein's *Battleship Potemkin,* a Russian entry from the silent era.

In 1992, seven years after Welles' death, the *Sight and Sound* list of ten greatest films became double-pronged, polling critics and directors separately. In both categories *Kane* placed number one. Next, in 1998, the American Film Institute issued a list of the hundred greatest films, on a vote by fifteen hundred top professionals. *Kane* led the way at number one. The latest poll, *Sight and Sound*'s list for 2002, still has *Kane* in the top spot, again favored by both directors and critics. With that, one commentator remarked that *Kane* had become "the Shakespeare of film," meaning that it has reached a level so lofty that it will likely never be dislodged.

A thankless reminder must here be added. These polls give the opinion of film professionals. Judged at the box office, a similar vote taken among the general public, ordinary movie-goers, would put *Kane* nowhere near the top. That undoubted fact points up a final reason for Welles' later failure: his work lacked sufficient commercial appeal, and the financiers knew it.

Appendix B
Citizen Kane *in Hearst* *Biography*

As might be expected, Hearst biographers since 1941, the year of *Kane,* tend to see things a bit differently from the rest of us.

Of the nine books published on Hearst since then, four are full, formal biographies, the others being more narrowly specialized works. Two of the four, however, those by Tebbel (1952) and Winkler (1955), were published while *Kane* was in eclipse. Winkler has nothing at all to say about *Kane*/Hearst, and Tebbel nothing of significance (an "ill-considered attempt to suppress the picture," in which Hearst "sat back and let Miss Parsons and his lawyer carry the assault").

In 1961, a decade after Hearst's death, W. A. Swanberg produced a readable, well-researched volume catchily entitled *Citizen Hearst.* Surprising everyone, it became a best-seller. Forty years later, in 2000, appeared an even more exhaustive and detailed effort, *The Chief,* by David Nasaw, which draws on documents not previously available.

The Swanberg book—despite its clever title which strongly points up the tie with the movie—on the matter of *Citizen Kane* is a disappointment. Only two of its six-hundred pages deal with the film and the old battle, and then in terms more than perfunctory. In the process it manages to mute, even excuse Hearst's part in what took place. While admitting that the picture "raised a cinematic storm," and while a few general details of the fight are supplied, Swanberg's own offhand comments betray his true sympathies. It is easy to understand, he remarks in summing up, why the aged tycoon objected "to having his own private life along with his wife and that of Miss Davies spread with thin concealment on the screen . . . this was hardly fair to Hearst, who in his better moments was kindliness itself."

In the frantic attempt by the Hearst forces to halt public showings of the movie, Hearst is kept by Swanberg well in the background. The lead in the theater lockout, he declares, was taken on their own by a phalanx of concerned moguls. "The pressure against the release of *Kane,*" writes Swanberg, "came from the top men in the industry who liked Hearst or feared the hurtful assault of his newspapers." The offer to buy *Kane* in order to destroy it—actually relayed to RKO by Louis Mayer *from* Hearst—is made to seem as if it came from the suddenly soft-hearted Mayer himself, anxiously concerned that Hearst's feelings might be hurt: "Louis Mayer, never a man to throw money away needlessly, showed remarkable loyalty to Hearst when he learned that the picture might wound his friend. Mayer offered to pay George Schaeffer, president of RKO, the $800,000 the film cost if he would destroy it." (Remarkable loyalty indeed!)

Though he fully concedes Hearst's journalistic depredations over the decades, rather obvious is Swanberg's sneaking admiration for his subject. His, in effect, airy dismissal of the *Kane* affair, brushing it aside as of little consequence, comes across as inevitable.

The Nasaw volume is different. Coming as it did after a great deal had been written by film critics and historians on the Welles-*Kane*-Hearst link—and particularly in Welles biographies by Leaming (1985), Brady (1989), Callow (1995), and Thomson (1996)—it could hardly avoid giving the topic extended treatment. This it does in en eleven-page chapter supported by another page of notes.

Reassuringly, the chapter opens with a display of knowledge as to how the picture in general was conceived and written (more or less accurate). But all too soon comes an observation so loose and unfounded that doubt is cast on everything said afterward. "It is possible that Welles was enough of a megalomaniac," writes Nasaw, "to believe that Hearst would be so entranced by seeing elements of his own life on the big screen that he would overlook the maliciously false portraits of the three women in his life." No, such a reaction is not possible, not for Welles, not for any person of intelligence.

Equally strange, the pliant Louella Parsons is seen by Nasaw as acting pretty much on her own, getting little or no direction from her boss. "Out of loyalty to Hearst," declares Nasaw, "sympathy for Marion, and loathing for Welles, Louella set out to destroy Welles. Hearst did nothing to stop her." Any biographer of Hearst—that fiercely controlling manipulator—who really believes that an underling would act in such a matter without the Chief's specific authorization is being less than perceptive.

Hearst does, in Nasaw's treatment, however, get the blame for *some* of what was done by the anti-Welles forces. The attempt to brand Welles as a communist because of his association with radio's Free Company came at Hearst's order, concedes the biographer (who himself gets in a belated dig at the unoffending Free Company members, styling them "a leftist group of writers and directors"). The shutting off of the necessary theater chain outlets owned by Hearst's fellow moguls, Nasaw also allows to be the work, not of the moguls themselves concerned about Hearst's "feelings," but of the angry, self-styled "Chief" himself.

That *Kane*'s failure at the box office was not wholly the result of Hearst's "retaliation," but only in part, Nasaw correctly concludes in quoting several of Welles' biographers and commentators (Callow, Carringer,

Thomson). That unexpected failure, he rightly states, was in large part a result of the movie's own lack of direct appeal for a mass audience.

But Nasaw is much too trusting (and selective) in his evaluation of other sources—not surprising, for his admiration of his subject is palpable, much as with Swanberg. Twice, for example, he asserts by allusion what is certainly not true, that Hearst never viewed the movie. Schaeffer at RKO, he writes, before the picture's release, "in a gesture of conciliation sent a print of the edited film to Hearst. It was returned with the seals unbroken." No proof exists that Schaeffer sent a print— hoping for "conciliation" by showing Hearst a film which left his personal reputation in tatters would have been, let us say, a doubtful procedure—but Nasaw supports the idea by quoting a Hearst reply to an interviewer's question. In it he claims to be "the only other guy in Hollywood who has not seen *Citizen Kane*. So I cannot discuss the picture." On this point Swanberg is the more accurate, agreeing with what is now conceded, that Hearst did view the movie, and maybe more than once. "Hearst was able," writes Swanberg, "to joke about *Citizen Kane*. 'We have it here,' he said. 'I must run it off again some time.'" Of course, the *joking* may be doubted.

Concluding, Nasaw honestly recognizes the one salient fact about *Kane* and the Chief which still has resonance. Latter-day viewers of the film, he writes candidly, "never having seen one of Marion's films or lived through Hearst's heyday as publisher and politician, had no reason to believe that the portrait was not an accurate one. . . . The lines between the fictional and the real have become so blurred that today, almost sixty years after the film was made, and a half-century since Hearst's death, it is difficult to disentangle the intermingled portraits of Charles Foster Kane and William Randolph Hearst. Both were powerful, both were enormously wealthy, both had big houses and big egos."

Still he can't help dwelling on the fact, as he sees it, that between the two men, the fictional figure and the real one, there were very large differences (true enough, yet of questionable force in the discussion): "Kane is a cartoon-like caricature of a man who is hollowed out on the inside, forlorn, defeated, solitary." Hearst, on the other hand, "never regarded himself as a failure, never recognized defeat. . . . He did not, at the end of his life, run away from the world to entomb himself in a vast, gloomy, art-choked hermitage."

Of course, in essence, that is exactly what Hearst *did* do. Not at the close of his life. All during it.

Ending his treatment of *Citizen Kane,* Nasaw quotes a confession from Orson Welles in which he admits that "the real story of Hearst is quite different from Kane's. And Hearst himself—as a *man,* I mean— was *very* different." The quotation is correct, Welles did say that, but not until forty winters had besieged his brow, chastening his temperament and gentling his memory. By then Welles was also willing to declare with a straight face that the nice-but-ordinary Marion Davies had in her prime ranked as one of the top comediennes "in the whole history of the screen. She would have been a star if Hearst had never happened." Nasaw overlooks that one.

Davies herself had little to say about *Kane*. On her death in 1961 she left behind only a single slight reference to the movie, a passing reference in some rambling reminiscences dictated in the years following Hearst's death (published 1975). It amounts to little more than a claim of indifference:

> I never saw the picture *Citizen Kane* but my sister Rose did, and she said, "I'll kill him, it's terrible." . . . W. R. never went to see *Citizen Kane* either. The Hearst newspapers put a ban on it as far as publicity went, but W. R. wasn't little that way . . . plenty of people talked about *Citizen Kane*. They would say that it was terrible and I had to go see it. But we never did. . . . I had no anger toward Orson Welles. After all, everybody is created to do their very best, and he probably thought that was his way to make money. Who was I to say I didn't like the way he did his picture? I was not built that way. I liked to keep the waters calm.

She also denied ever meeting Aldous Huxley, or reading his novel, *After Many A Summer Dies the Swan,* published four years before *Kane:* "I heard about Aldous Huxley. I don't think I ever met him, nor did I read his book, but I wanted to." If anything is certain in the *Kane* affair it is that Hearst and his mistress not only saw the picture, but read the novel, and both certainly did meet Huxley.

Ten years after Davies' death there appeared a separate, formal biography of her, by Fred Guiles. A highly sympathetic treatment, its discussion of *Citizen Kane* is negligible, resting on a quick perusal of sources. The movie it takes note of mostly in relation to its portrait of Susan Alexander, Kane's pathetically doomed second wife (for the film, wife she had to be, not mistress). Repeatedly and resentfully, Guiles states his firm belief that *Kane* "destroyed" what he sees as Marion's lofty reputation as an actress. Its effect on her well-earned screen laurels after a long, hard career had been "murderous," he laments in apparent genuine sorrow.

Hearst he pictures as "devastated" by *Kane*'s treatment of Marion, describing him as "an old man trembling with indignation over the way they had handled his mistress in the film." Probably that was true, but Guiles' pity for the trembling old man was not shared by those aware of how often, and with how much less reason, that old man had caused others to tremble.

Marion herself, says Guiles, always "pretended that *[Kane]* didn't bother her," but it did, weighing down her last years. "None of Marion's friends would dare discuss even the film's existence. It had become taboo like death itself."

Lastly, it can bear repeating, no Hearst biographer so much as refers in passing to one of the starkest episodes in the story, Hearst's belated attack on Herman

Mankiewicz over the drunk driving incident (see above 189–94). Certainly Mankiewicz was at fault in the accident—which left no one badly hurt—and should have been held to proper account. What stands out as grotesquely revealing is Hearst's wildly excessive effort to brand him with permanent, public disgrace. The very real possibility that Hearst may have been responsible for what happened to Dorothy Commingore (see above 195–203) is also ignored by Hearst's chroniclers.

Notes and Sources

Along with source citations, these notes offer added comment on various significant items in the text, as well as some more rarified or tangential. Sources are given in shortened form and may be fully identified by a glance at the bibliography. Numbers down the left margin indicate *pages* in the text above.

Prologue: His Hour

xiii   Citizen Kane *and the polls:* See Appendix A.

xiv   Kane *at the box office:* That the movie failed to make a profit during its four-month run in 1941 is an admitted fact. For further discussion see below, 272.

xviii   *Rosebud as symbol:* Welles himself often deprecated this one-word denouement of his film as a mere gimmick. "Dollar-book Freud," he branded it (while pointedly crediting its origin to Mankiewicz). But surely Welles knew better than that, for in the film *it works,* and perfectly. Anything more profound or abstruse would have seriously lamed that precisely managed socko ending.

xx "the word *genius* was whispered"—Leaming, 178, see
also the *Los Angeles Times,* October 10, 1985. Except
perhaps for the remarkable *breadth* of his talents,
Welles cannot really be considered a genius in the formal sense of the term. Certainly he possessed ingenuity of a very high order, especially when he had existing materials to work with. Nor was he original in the
absolute sense, but was a marvelously capable adapter
and refiner of other men's work. This was true of him
as both a writer and director, and, curiously, as actor.
His true creative flair was a wonderfully acute sense of
theater, an unerring instinct for the compelling moment emphasized. "It is no denigration of Welles' talent," commented John Houseman, the colleague who
perhaps knew him best, "to observe that throughout
his career he had functioned most effectively and
created most freely when he was supported by a
strong text. . . . His ability to push a dramatic situation far beyond its normal level of tension made him a
great director but an inferior dramatist. His story
sense was erratic and disorganized; whenever he
strayed outside the solid structure of someone else's
work he ended in formless confusion. But this was
something his ego would not acknowledge" (*Run-
Through,* 459–60).

Chapter 1. Sneak Preview

3 *Hedda Hopper:* Hopper's attendance at the screening is
in her *From Under My Hat,* 289–90. My text draws
out the obvious implications buried in that brief account. See also her *Whole Truth,* 69–70. Later she
claimed to have been on the *Kane* set several times
while shooting was in progress, and "anyone with
half an eye could see that the story bore a striking resemblance to Mr. Hearst's life" (*Whole Truth,* 289).

But that was hindsight, for Welles was very careful with visitors to his closed set—there were a few, all by invitation—to be at work on something innocuous.

4   Kane *screening of January 1941:* Brady, 273–74; Callow, 530–31; Higham, *Orson Welles,* 168; Leaming, 205. The stories and reviews written by two of the invited journalists appeared in *Life,* March 14, 1941, and *Look,* March 17, 1941. Douglas Churchill wrote no formal review or story about the movie.

6   "Few movies have ever come from Hollywood"—*Life,* March 14, 1941.

7   "Old-fashioned . . . very corny"—Brady, 274. Though at this juncture Hopper was a strong Hearst partisan, she later distanced herself from the fray, praising Welles: "The boy who was spat upon, jeered, and ridiculed, has made the town swallow its words" (*San Francisco Chronicle,* May 13, 1941).

7   "appalled"—Hopper, *Whole Truth,* 69. See also Hopper, *From Under My Hat,* 289–92.

7   "always been unfailingly kind"—Hopper, *From Under My Hat,* 290.

7   *Hopper and Welles in New York City:* Hopper, *Whole Truth,* 69, *From Under My Hat,* 289. Hopper had known Welles, she says, "ever since I'd been a struggling actress [in New York] and he'd gone out of his way to be kind to my son Bill, who was a struggling young actor" (*Whole Truth,* 69). In her other book she tells a bit more: "My friendship with Orson goes back to the time my son Bill was doing a walk-on in *Romeo and Juliet* with Katharine Cornell, Basil Rathbone, and Orson in New York. . . . I was a struggling actress and appreciated a stranger taking time out to help my rough recruit of a son. Bill introduced us one night at supper at the Algonquin Hotel. . . . I liked him. We argue; we've even had some rough skirmishes. But I

can't resist him" (*From Under My Hat*, 289). Welles played Mercutio in *Romeo and Juliet*, with Cornell in the lead, in 1933–34, including a nationwide tour after the New York opening.

9   "am impudent, murderous trick . . . Cockiness I can take"—Hopper, *From Under My Hat*, 290.

Chapter 2. Boy Wonder

11   *The Chateau Marmont:* Welles' original registration card is given as an illustration in Sarlot and Basten, as is that of John Houseman. The Marmont is still in operation, not so exclusive as it once was, but very proud of its star-studded past.

11   *Welles' arrival in Hollywood:* Brady, 201; Callow, 457–58.

12   *The Martian scare:* The full story is now available in *Invasion from Mars* by Hadley Cantril. For a more recent treatment in some detail see Brady, 162–80.

15   *Welles' earlier career:* Fowler, 31–57; Callow, 150–350; Brady, 64–185. Perhaps someday there will be a book focused wholly on Welles' earliest stage and radio career, say from age sixteen to twenty-four. It eminently deserves it, if for its sheer unlikely youthful ambition and drama alone.

15   "Marvelous Boy"—*Time,* May 9, 1938. The article also gives a fairly detailed sketch of Welles' life and career to that point, apparently the first to do so.

16   *Shadow to Shakespeare:* On radio during 1938 and 1939 Welles played the lead in the popular suspense drama *The Shadow*. It was his voice that each week intoned those memorable phrases—now curiously applicable to *Citizen Kane*—"Who knows what evil lurks in the hearts of men? *The Shadow* knows!" Sinister laughter follows the confident declaration.

17   *Welles' RKO contract:* Brady, 199–201, rests on a study of the document itself, unlike some other commentators. See also *Time,* July 31, 1939, and the *New York Times,* August 20, 1939. It's not too much to say that this was and remains the most extraordinary Hollywood contract *ever,* even aside from Welles' youth and inexperience. It amounted to handing him sole responsibility for some $1.5 million. See also Callow, 451–53.

20   "There's no use looking"—John Koenig as quoted in Brady, 214.

23   "John Ford was my teacher"—Powell. It appears that most, by far, of Welles' time while studying moviemaking was spent watching and analyzing films. See Brady, 209, and Lebo, 89.

23   "This is the biggest electric train set"—Brady, 208, no specific source cited, whether in print or oral.

24   "A genius is a crackpot"—*Daily Variety,* August 23, 1939.

24   *Welles' visit to Shirley Temple:* Leaming, 171; Black, 283–85. The *New York Times* photograph of the two—at that moment the world's best-known American male and female!—appeared on August 20, 1939. The caption refers to Welles as "The Man from Mars."

24   "he expressed himself"—*New York Times,* August 20, 1939.

25   *Little Orson Annie:* First printed as part of a story on Welles in the *New York Times,* January 28, 1940 ("A Week of Orson Welles"). The author is identified as the actor Gene Lockhart. I give the verse as quatrains rather than as the newspaper's long-line couplets, which read very clumsily.

25   "concentrated malice"—Callow, 458.

26   "an elegant little folio"—*New York Times,* January 28, 1940. The story describes the folio (booklet) as "bound almost as elaborately as *A Treasury of Art Masterpieces.*"

26   "Orson Welles . . . spectacular genius"— *Variety,* August 17, 1939. This ad, of course, was an official announcement to the trade. The first public announcement had come a month earlier in *Time.*

26   "a holdout against Hollywood's"— *Time,* July 31, 1939.

27   "The announcement of the Conrad work"—*New York Times,* August 20, 1939.

27   *The Campbell Playhouse:* Brady, 179–85, and Callow, 418–23, 460–63. For whatever reason, the series was not renewed in the spring of 1940.

29   "The effect of war"— *Time,* September 18, 1939. For some discussion of Hollywood's overseas markets and the effect on them of war, see Brady, 215–16.

30   *Cancellation of* Darkness—Callow, 469–76; Brady, 213–16.

31   "Mrs. Orson Welles to sue"—*New York Times,* December 16, 1939.

31   "had been seen frequently"—*New York Times,* January 18, 1940.

32   *The dinner at Chasen's:* Houseman, *Run-Through,* 437–40; Callow, 447–48; Brady, 235; Leaming, 184. Welles' ugly mood that night is made quite plain in the sources.

35   "We have been through too much"— Houseman, *Run-Through,* 440. The "situation" he refers to concerned what he calls "My false position with the Mercury [Players]." Inevitably, Houseman tended to wilt in the fairly consuming heat of the Welles talent and temperament.

36   "They are laying bets"—*Hollywood Reporter,* January 8, 1940, as quoted in Thomson, 136.

36 "There are different estimates of Welles"—*Saturday Evening Post,* January 20, 1940. The second and third parts appeared in subsequent weeks, on January 27 and February 3. The lengthy, well illustrated series offered the fullest, most detailed biography of Welles to then. Its first installment opens: "Orson Welles, the boy who raised gooseflesh on a continent with his Martian monsters, received his first important publicity in 1925, when he was ten years old. A newspaper of Madison, Wisconsin, printed a column about him under the headline, *A Poet, Artist, Cartoonist and Actor at 10 Years.*" A picture of the old column from the *Wisconsin State Journal* accompanies the *Post* text (the headline actually reads, "Cartoonist, Actor, Poet, and Only 10").

Chapter 3. Aging Wonder

37 *Hearst's office at San Simeon:* Based on photographs and descriptions of San Simeon in Murray, Lewis, and a 1965 tourists' brochure.

39 *Hearst properties*—For some of these properties Hearst's ownership was not absolute, having been diluted after a financial crisis in 1937. His personal influence, however, had not been diminished in the least, nor had his ruthless outlook on men and events.

40 *Hearst background:* The following ten volumes, together, provide a rounded portrait of Hearst, including his shortcomings and his all too few virtues: Nasaw, Procter, Swanberg, Tebbel, Lundberg, Carlson/Bates, Winkler, Older, Guiles, and Davies. Nasaw, notably sympathetic, is the most thorough. Swanberg is the most readable, also sympathetic but candid.

41 "Regular readers of a Hearst paper"—Swanberg, 234. More specifically, but still lightly and with a note of

amused tolerance, Swanberg sketches several of the methods by which Hearst prostituted his newspapers: "He had few scruples about the sanctity of the news and would cheer a story containing manufactured shock, and frown at one containing only dull fact. The pressure for shock caused writers to stretch fact to the bursting point, to stress some angle out of all semblance to its true significance, and often to bolster a commonplace story with delicate fabrication. Murder, adultery, and scandal were sure front-page material, and newsmen on other sheets were cynically amused at the ability of the Hearst men to discover 'secret diaries,' and other astonishing sidelights in these cases which the most diligent search by competing reporters had failed to uncover. To be a Hearst reporter required talents unsought by sober journals—a lively imagination, a fictional sense that could touch up news stories with vivid glints. . . . A Hearst headline writer was a specialist in condensed shock, seizing on the most fantastic facet in any story and compressing it into a capsule jolt" (233).

Probably it is now too late for the exhaustive study of Hearst's journalistic depredations that cries out to be made—compiling a detailed catalogue of his newspapers' sixty years of deceit, imposition, fraud, and actual lawbreaking, in large matters and small. The necessary research, in the old newspapers and the backgrounds of the relevant stories, is probably now beyond the reach of any one man, so it is unlikely that the true extent and nature of his guilt will ever be known. The present tendency, in fact, is quite the opposite. Now there is a rush to "understand" and largely excuse (with a shrug and a smile—see Swanberg and Nasaw) even the more glaring Hearstian scandals.

One prominent and rather disconcerting example of this revisionist tendency is the 1998 volume by Ben Procter, covering Hearst's "Early Years: 1863–1910." Based on extensive original research in two Hearst papers, the *San Francisco Examiner* and the *New York Morning Journal,* the book has literally *nothing* to say about Hearst's admitted sins of journalistic corruption. Instead, it talks about his "imaginative showmanship and creative genius . . . his journalistic creativity and imaginative talent" (106, 112), and describes how he succeeded in adding "to the prevailing excitement . . . by encouraging ingenuity and creativeness" (87) in his reporters, writers, and editors.

Treating Hearst's role in the assassination of President McKinley (167–68), the Procter book entirely avoids quoting the one damning sentence from a Hearst editorial that caused most of the trouble ("If bad institutions and bad men cannot be got rid of except by killing, then the killing must be done"—see above 42 and three notes down). Then he decries the resulting public anger over McKinley's death that was directed at Hearst, dismissing it as "a crescendo of venomous censure and verbal invective" (167). Rather naively, Procter explains that he wrote the biography because the Hearst story "excites me," because Hearst "affected the lives of the American people," and because "his papers were wonderfully exciting and good reading, challenging and innovative and entertaining" (x). Almost, the book has about it the air of something authorized by the Hearst family, except that the author is a respected historian, a professor at Texas Christian University, and the book was published by Oxford University Press.

Some Hearst apologists like to credit him with ushering in the modern style of journalism. But of course modern media practices would have arrived without Hearst—granted, at a slower pace—and we might have been spared some of its excesses.

41 "He preaches the gospel"—Nasaw, 210, quoting a Roosevelt letter.

41 "No other press lord"—*Time,* March 11, 1939.

42 "If bad institutions"—*New York Evening Journal,* April 10, 1901; See Carlson/Bates, 112; Swanberg, 227–30; Lungberg, 89; and Nasaw, 156–58. Lungberg, 88–89, reports an earlier Hearst editorial in the *Evening Journal* actually advocating political assassination. The McKinley assassination (transferred to a fictional president), and the Hearst role in it, was originally a part of the *Kane* script. In fact the sequence was shot, but was later dropped. See Carringer, "Scripts of *Citizen Kane,*" 152; Kael, 60; Lebo, 156.

43 *Marion Davies:* Guiles gives a full and generally reliable portrait, but where her acting talent is concerned making much of little. Though apparently a likeable woman, except for her connection with Hearst she hardly rates a full-scale biography. Everyone now tends to see her in a sympathetic light, even Orson Welles succumbing. In a foreword he supplied for her 1975 autobiography, a sketchy account published after her death, he actually says that between the two women, Marion and Susan in *Kane,* there was "no resemblance at all," and he even gives her acting high praise, calling her "one of the most delightfully accomplished comediennes" in movie annals. Well, why not? By then what did it matter? Saying so probably made *him* feel better. In *Kane* he did come down pretty hard on poor Marion, of course a case of exaggeration for the sake of emphasis. Unlike Susan, Marion had *some* talent.

44   "After playing the eye-batting ingenue"—*New York
      Times,* July 2, 1937, as quoted in Guiles, 404. Twenty
      years earlier in reviewing her second silent film, the
      Times had been just as tepid: "There is no objection to
      Miss Davies. She is by no means a sensational screen
      actress, but she fills the requirements of her part"
      (Guiles, 376).

44   "When I was young"—Davies, 261. On the death of
      Hearst in 1951 she wasted no more time. At age fifty-
      four, having become an extremely rich woman, some
      two months after the Hearst funeral she married one
      Horace Brown, a ship's captain in the merchant ma-
      rine. It is thought that she had known him for some
      time.

48   *San Simeon:* The Murray book, *Golden Days at San
      Simeon* (foreword by Ronald Reagan, then California
      governor), gives the fullest picture. See also the bro-
      chure by Lewis.

48   "a most surprising sight . . . in a kind of stony
      efflourescence"—Huxley, 18–20. Curiously, in her de-
      finitive, almost eight-hundred-page biography of
      Huxley, Bedford has only a single passing reference to
      Hearst, barely acknowledging a possible link between
      After Many a Summer and the tycoon, his mistress,
      and his castle.

49   *Aldous Huxley background:* Bedford, Clark, and Duna-
      way. In Welles and Hearst biography Huxley is never
      mentioned more than casually, the link with his novel,
      After Many a Summer Dies the Swan, getting a mere
      nod. As early as September 1922 Huxley's story *The
      Gioconda Smile* appeared in *Hearst's Magazine.*

50   "You asked for it"—Huxley, 48–51. That this passage
      reflects Huxley's own experience on an early visit to
      San Simeon is my own conclusion.

53   "He will depart loved by few"—Lundberg, vii.

53   "William Randolph Hearst's career"—ibid., 380–81.

54   "His flaunting in the face"—Carlson/Bates, xiv–xv.

54   "a new interest to divert . . . His successful flouting"—ibid., 194.

54   "Not only is she the only star"—ibid., 196. When the Carlson/Bates volume came out Miss Davies was engaged in making what would prove to be her final screen appearance, *Ever Since Eve*. In retirement she continued to be listed as president of Cosmopolitan Pictures.

55   "discovered . . . find . . . photographed and interviewed"—ibid.

55   "With the power that moves mountains"—ibid., 305.

57   "hangs in Miss Davies' bedroom . . . He has collected"—ibid. The effective phrase "loot from all the world," used by Carlson/Bates to describe the San Simeon treasures, was borrowed by Mankiewicz for the *Citizen Kane* script. It occurs in the *News On the March* sequence where the narrator tells of the "Contents of Xanadu's palace . . . the loot of the world."

57   "with stooped shoulders . . . The unmentioned"—ibid., 311–12.

58   *The Ince affair:* The fullest treatment, a bit surprisingly, occurs not in Hearst biography but in the Guiles biography of Marion Davies (154–62). Davies herself refers to it in her autobiography, *Times We Had*, 65–67, 260. Among Hearst biographers it is briefly covered by Nasaw, 344–45; Swanberg, 445–46; and Carlson/Bates, 198–201. Winkler and Older don't mention it, nor does Lundberg, in keeping with his decision not to treat private matters.

60   "trying with a pocket handkerchief"—Huxley, 314.

61   "I'll make it worth your while"—ibid., 317–18. The presence of the Ince affair in the background of the

Huxley novel has been noticed, but in passing. In his account of Huxley's Hollywood period, Dunaway refers to the Ince matter and lightly comments: "Whether or not Hearst slipped something into his consommé is irrelevant; few were better positioned to get away with murder—a fact Huxley duly noted for the climax of *Swan*. After Ince's death becoming Marion Davies' lover grew less fashionable" (81). Robert Baker in his respected volume of Huxley criticism, *The Dark Historic Page*, gives an entire chapter, some thirty pages, to *After Many a Summer*, without at all acknowledging the Hearst connection. Discussion of a novel as variously disputed and estimated as this one would only benefit from a recognition of its real-life background.

62 *Welles attends the Huxley party:* Bedford, 381; Dunaway, 120–21; Friedrich, 27. Apparently the party was to celebrate Huxley's birthday as well as the completion of his novel. Neither source notes that Welles and Huxley at the party had any private talk about *Summer*. That is my own conclusion, not so wild a one, I submit. What may have been the prior link between the two men, that led to the invitation, I have not been able to discover. Later Huxley did some scriptwriting for the movie *Jane Eyre* (1942), which starred Welles.

Chapter 4. Conjuring *Kane*

63 *Mankiewicz background:* The only Mankiewicz biography, that by Meryman, is a very sympathetic treatment but full and detailed. He also gets fairly extensive notice in the Geist biography of his brother Joseph, as well as in Houseman, *Run-Through*. See also Brady, 233–34; Callow, 482–84; Kael, 10–12, 15, 20–24, 29–31. Specific references to his work on *Citizen Kane* appear below.

66   *The accident:* Meryman, 239–40; Lebo, 12–13; Brady, 234; Houseman, *Run-Through,* 448. The car belonged to Phipps, who'd offered Mank a ride.

67   *The genesis of* Kane: The writing of the *Citizen Kane* script—it went through seven revisions—has been much discussed, the modern phase kicked off by Pauline Kael's 1971 *New Yorker* piece, which argues for Mank's precedence. Today the clash of opinion about the who and the how of it still sounds, the question still largely unsettled. "Almost impossible to trace," is how Welles' most recent and most complete biographer views the whole matter (Brady, 230). But that's being far too pessimistic. Patient analysis of the sources, which are not few and are readily available, yields the pattern of events detailed in this chapter, a pattern which will, I feel, prove to be as close to the truth as we are likely to get. A detail here or there may be argued, but not the general design.

68   "vying with each other"—Houseman to Mrs. Mankiewicz, quoted in Brady, 234.

71   *Reception of the Huxley novel:* The number of copies sold is in Bedford, 390. In his account of Huxley's Hollywood stay, biographer Dunaway, concerning the publication of *After Many a Summer,* observes, "Considering Huxley had lambasted one of America's most powerful financiers . . . the mystery is why he never suffered the fate of Orson Welles and Herman Mankiewicz after *Citizen Kane* appeared. . . . If Hearst would be this furious at *Kane,* how did Huxley get away with *Swan*?" (53). Then he lets the question go largely unanswered, venturing only that Huxley's boss at MGM, Louis Mayer, had fallen out with Hearst—which in itself was not true. The reason that the Huxley novel was not targeted by Hearst is rather obviously the one I suggest.

72   "is an Asiatically splendiferous"—Fadiman, 33.

73   "A picture based on the Huxley"—These conjectured words of Mankiewicz begin the section of my text which presents in narrative form what I conceive to have been the actual birth of the *Kane* concept (as distinguished from the writing of the script). It draws on primary information available in the following sources: Carringer, "Scripts"; Carringer, *Making,* 16–18; Meryman, 235–49; Lebo, 33–36; Houseman, *Run-Through,* 448–49; Kael, 33–36; Brady, 230–36; Callow, 482–87; Rosenbaum, 58–60; and Leaming, 183. More specific citations are given below.

75   The Power and the Glory: A Fox film released in 1933, written by Preston Sturges, directed by William Howard, starring a very young Spencer Tracy. A ruthless, self-made railroad president kills himself and his life is uncovered in several revealing flashbacks centered on his secretary. Years later Welles was asked whether the picture had influenced *Kane.* He denied having seen it, and in this case—not always!—I'm inclined to believe him: "No, I never saw it. I've heard that it has strong similarities; it's one of those coincidences. I'm a great fan of Sturges and I'm grateful I didn't see it. He never accused me of it—we were great chums—but I just never saw it" (Rosenbaum, 61). On the other hand, Mankiewicz, whether or not telling Welles about it at the time, I feel sure both saw the picture and, for *Kane,* made deliberate use of its nonlinear flashback method. Carringer (*Making,* 18) concedes the link but insists that *Kane*'s flashback technique is much superior (certainly true). The discussion in Kael (36, 50, 75) leaves little doubt of the picture's direct influence on *Kane.*

78   *Mankiewicz's first short treatment of* Kane: For this I give the opening sequence as it appears in the first of

the seven script versions (Brady, 237–38; Carringer, "Scripts," 143). Carringer also shows that originally the word Rosebud was to have been uttered by the dying Kane not once but repeatedly.

78 *Origin of Rosebud:* That both the word and its symbolism was the creation of Mankiewicz was early conceded by Welles (Meryman, 250; Thomson, 137; Higham, *Orson Welles,* 153). That the word bore for Hearst an intimate personal application to Marion is found in several sources: for an extended discussion see Bates, 197–99. The idea that Mankiewicz heard the story from actress Louise Brooks at San Simeon first occurs in Anger (159), a highly plausible suggestion. Brooks was Davies' closest female friend and longtime confidante. If it was not Brooks then other possibilities are two other close friends, screenwriter Anita Loos and actress Bebe Daniels. A remoter possibility is the writer Aldous Huxley, who was a good friend of Anita Loos, though whether he and Mankiewicz ever met is uncertain. Making the whole story yet more probable is the fact, developed by Bates, that in Victorian low-life slang the word rosebud is often found referring to the female genitalia. The spoken exchange between Welles and his collaborator in this scene derives from close study of all the sources listed above.

81 *The writing contract and credits:* The contract that Mankiewicz signed with Welles states that Mercury Productions—meaning Welles—"shall be deemed author and creator" of the script—meaning that Mankiewicz would not (or need not) be named. Yet the scriptwriting credit on the finished film *does* include him, in fact lists his name first, above that of Welles, who of course had the final say. How that result came about has generated a separate argument, still not quite settled. Welles' own claim that, despite the contract, he

had always intended to credit his cowriter has been vigorously disputed. The disgruntled Mankiewicz, it is pointed out, having changed his mind about not getting credit, actually appealed for redress to the Screen Writers Guild (it declined to act in the matter).

Earlier, according to internal memos by publicity man Herbert Drake to Welles (August 26 and September 5, 1940, originals in the Orson Welles Papers, Lilly Library, Indiana University), Mankiewicz had demanded that Welles stop his verbal claims, in interviews, about being *Kane*'s author. If Welles kept it up, threatened Mankiewicz, he'd take a full-page ad in the trade papers denying it, would give a story to the wire services, and would get his friend Ben Hecht to write an article for the *Saturday Evening Post* exposing Welles' pretensions (Drake's listing of these items appears serious but it's not easy to be sure). Then a few days after that outburst a contrite Mankiewicz took it all back, or so Drake reports in another memo to Welles: "Mankiewicz says the last thing he wants is for us to write any stories indicating he is the author of *Citizen Kane,* co-author, or had any connection with it. He said he realizes completely that we can't stop the result of a year's four-ply publicity. He will take no action when such things appear. What he wants is simply this, he asks that you don't in a personal interview say that you wrote *Citizen Kane.*"

In all of this, the only thing certain is that, legally, Welles didn't have to do what he did in sharing the credit. For some sense of the basic elements in the argument see Meryman, 263–66; Callow, 517–19; Kael, 37–39; Carringer, *Making,* 31–33; Brady, 236–40; and Houseman, *Run-Through,* 459–60.

82 *The writing of* Citizen Kane: This is and has long been an active field of study, with opinions especially as to its

beginnings differing rather wildly. My view rests on information found in several sources: Carringer, *Making,* 141–71; Carringer, "Scripts," 16–35; Brady, 230–51; Meryman, 248–58; Houseman, *Run-Through,* 447–58; Thomson, 145–48; and Kael. Mankiewicz tended to see himself as sole original creator, claiming that the concept grew out of some of his own earlier movie ideas. But I am convinced that it all began with Welles thinking he'd film the Huxley novel, and it was at a later point that Mankiewicz suggested they do an original story. No prior discussion of the topic, so far as I can find, recognizes the Huxley book's pivotal place in the genesis of *Kane.*

84   "We set out for the San Bernardino mountains"— Houseman, *Run-Through,* 450–51. Houseman's rather sly reference to "research material," not further explained, of course means *Hearst* research, and the materials certainly included the two recent biographies of Hearst, by Lundberg and Carlson/Bates, as well as the Huxley novel, and the earlier biographies by Older and Winkler. The two men also made good use of the extensive bibliographies in these biographies, listing books and articles on Hearst and related matters.

Both Welles and Mankiewicz afterwards denied using published sources, of course an inevitable stance at the time. Today it is conceded by all that the movie certainly draws on any number of published sources. Mankiewicz in 1943 privately admitted that he "knew more about Hearst than any man alive," and that before writing *Kane* he studied Hearst's career "like a scholar" (Kael, 80; see also Meryman, 249–51).

In 1950 Lundberg brought a plagiarism suit against RKO over *Kane.* The case was eventually settled out of court, with the studio paying a $15,000 award to the complainant and assuming all court costs (Kael, 81–82; Meryman, 256; Lebo, 160; Carringer, *Making,* 21–23). During the trial it was shown from Mankiewicz's own records that he owned no fewer than four copies of the Lundberg book. Even then he maintained that he hadn't read it, at least couldn't remember doing so (Houseman, *Front and Center,* 333–34).

The Carlson/Bates volume, so obviously a source for *Kane,* has not previously been noted in this connection. It would seem that a full-scale study of *Kane*'s sources should be the next order of business on the agenda of serious *Kane*/Welles scholars. The work already done along this line is extensive, but disconnected and desultory.

85 "having made an enormous production"—Houseman, *Run-Through,* 455.

85 "We were not entirely incommunicado "—ibid., 455–56. Houseman recalled only one visit by Welles during the ten weeks of writing. Other sources put him there several times. For a photograph of all three men together at Victorville conferring on the *Kane* script (Welles, Mankiewicz, Houseman), see above, 83.

87 "the narrative brilliance"—Carringer, *Making,* 35. The question of Welles' contribution to the *Kane* script has come to form almost a separate formal study of its own. For some discussion see Meryman, 251–60; Lebo, 26–31; Gottesman, *Perspectives,* 94–121, 141–73, 268–94, 383–429, 527–68; Kael, 33–41, 49–51; and Brady, 235–46.

87 *RKO approval of the script:* Strangely, the studio's final approval, surely an essential part of *Kane*'s history, is nowhere explicitly discussed. Closest are Callow, 495, and Kael, 59.

Chapter 5. On the Set

89   "We're only making tests"—Lebo, 73; Callow, 507; Rosenbaum, 93.

90   "Mr. Welles is conducting"—*New York Times,* as quoted in Brady, 252, no date.

91   "was indeed the most exciting"—Toland, "Cameraman," 650.

92   "He proved one of the most"—ibid.

92   "should go hang . . . where most cinematographers"—Toland, "How I Broke," 569.

92   "he came to the job"—ibid.

94   "went on for twenty-four hours"—Leaming, 180. Same for the next quote in this paragraph.

94   "One day on a scene"—ibid, 182.

95   "There are more conscious shots"—Rosenbaum, 542.

96   "On the day we were there"—*San Francisco Chronicle,* March 16, 1941, magazine section, 18. The reporter was Charles Escourt.

98   "marvelously exciting"—Lebo, xiv. The colleague was Robert Wise.

98   *Visits to the set by Parsons and Hopper:* Parsons, *Tell It,* 131; Hopper, *From Under My Hat,* 290; Eells, 211; *Time,* January 27, 1941. A letter of Mankiewicz (Meryman, 267) supposedly refers to these visits. But as usual Mank is only being clever, not conveying fact.

98   "he photographs like a million dollars"—Quoted in Higham, *Orson Welles,* 159.

98   "It deals with a dead man"—ibid, 163.

99   *Impossible to prevent talk:* As she herself confessed years later, one of those who talked was Ruth Warrick, who played the first wife in *Kane.* Interviewed for the volume *Forties Film Talk,* she explained that on a brief visit to her Connecticut home in late 1940 while the picture was still shooting, she was asked by RKO to

give an interview to a New York paper, identified as *PM*. When the reporter asked what the movie "was all about," Warrick replied: "I told him what Orson had told me," that it was the story of "all the men who became our heroes and then turned into the despoilers of America—men like Hearst. . . . He never let me finish. I was going to mention several others. He suddenly doubled up as if he'd been poisoned, said, 'Excuse me,' and hurried away. The next day everything hit the fan. The article reported that I had said the movie was about Hearst. This was the first that this had been in print. I thought, this is the end of me. The picture had been booked into Radio City Music Hall but was now pulled from there" (McClelland, 185).

It's very unlikely that she was first to reveal the secret, which would mean before the *Newsweek* item on September 16, 1940 (see two notes below). More likely it happened between that date and December or early January. (A quick look at the August–September *PM* failed to find the story. On August 2 the paper did carry a striking, full-page photograph of Welles in action as director on the *Kane* set.) If it all happened just as Warrick recalled, and the paper was indeed *PM,* the story should eventually turn up.

Another, even more likely source for early leaks about the Hearst link—probably the earliest and in the case very deliberate—was Welles' publicity man, Herbert Drake. An obscure figure little noticed in *Kane* literature, Drake was at the center of things from the start, as Welles' right hand in all relating to the flow of information on the picture. One of his letters contains a two-sentence statement which pretty surely identifies him as first breathing the name of Hearst in public. Writing to a friend in New York in October 1940, he complains archly: "The RKO executives have been told I precipitated the Hearst thing by announcing generally that *Kane* is the life of Hearst. This is, of course, a dirty lie, a base canard, a vile accusation, a vicious flight into the realms of imagination" (Brady, 265).

In giving that quote, biographer Brady correctly takes the tongue-in-cheek denial to be a confession of guilt, a playful admission by Drake that he did indeed "precipitate the Hearst thing." Comments Brady: "Although it has been denied by Welles, it is altogether possible that he had Drake, his press agent, trickle to the press by nuance, and perhaps a whisper to an attentive ear," the notion that Kane was Hearst. "The publicity possibilities," adds Brady, "of a mischievous controversy—Hearst threatening a suit—were enormous" (265).

100 *The Lederer script incident:* Unlike my version, the standard presentation of this peculiar episode has Mankiewicz, stupidly and against all reason, giving a copy of the *actual Kane* script to his friend Lederer. Supposedly, Lederer read it, then blithely handed it back, saying it was OK and wouldn't disturb anyone at San Simeon (Meryman, 269; see also Kael, 45, and Brady, 272). But that simply *can't* be the truth. Aside from everything else, Welles planned for the fuss with Hearst to start *after* the movie was made, not before. If the true script had been seen at San Simeon, an explosion would have resulted, with the Hearst battery of lawyers jumping to attack, their first move a restraining order. Early intimidated, *Kane* would probably never have been made.

Complicating the picture somewhat is a letter written by Lederer a few weeks before he was given the script to read. Dated June 22, 1940, it shows that relations between him and Welles' lawyer, Arnold

Weissberger, were downright hostile, the implication being that the hostility extended to Weissberger's client. According to the letter (unpublished) the lawyer had accused Lederer, for reasons not specific, of being "uncivil and belligerent." Lederer does not deny the charge, but proceeds to justify it: "I have never been able to resist assuming such an attitude when I encounter what seems to me villainy" (from the original in the Orson Welles Papers, Lilly Library, Indiana University). What the "villainy" may have been is neither explained nor hinted, but the word of course would serve very well as a description of *Kane* from the Hearst side. This openly unfriendly exchange just before Lederer was given the spurious *Kane* script to read suggests that *something* untoward was going on. Perhaps the supplying of the doctored script was done not so much as a stunt, but under the pressure of a demand. Perhaps Lederer had heard rumors about *Kane*'s premise, then about to start filming. That rumor *may* have been that *Kane*'s plot incorporated elements of the Huxley novel.

100   "The script of Orson Welles' first movie"—*Newsweek*, September 16, 1940. That is the whole extent of the item. It is dropped into a catch-all column on page 12 without preparation or comment. The source may have been Welles' publicity man Herbert Drake, who was behind all the journalistic coverage of *Kane* (see his memo to Welles, dated October 4, 1940, in the Orson Welles Papers, Lilly Library, Indiana University).

101   "It is a portrait"—Gottesman, *Focus,* 68.

Chapter 6. Stranded

103   "Chief, it's me"—Hopper's phone conversation with Hearst took place on the morning after she viewed the film at RKO on January 3, 1941. Her record of the call, all too brief, is in her *From Under My Hat,* 290, and

Whole Truth, 70. What she said to Hearst isn't detailed, but from what she does say, and in light of what happened afterwards, the *content* of her report becomes quite evident, if not the actual words she used. Especially, I think, she *must* have asked about the word Rosebud, as I show her doing, guided by her well-honed instincts as a gossip columnist.

Her bringing up the passage in the Huxley novel (*After Many a Summer,* 307) in which Stoyte smashes up a room, as the basis for Kane's similar action in Susan's bedroom, I think is eminently justified. The reason given in the novel for the destruction is different, and the room is not a bedroom, but otherwise the link is striking. With only a change of the objects smashed, the Huxley passage might almost be taken as detailing the action in *Kane,* especially when compared with the relevant passage in the actual script (available in Kael, 279–85). The scene as shot is a bit more elaborate.

105   *Parsons' background:* Parsons *Gay Illiterate* and *Tell It;* Eells; Brady, 180, 266; Callow, 473–74.

107   "expected to find a haughty star"—Parsons, *Gay Illiterate,* 102.

107   "Where are the words"—ibid., 84.

108   "the gayest and best occasions . . . the love and good wishes"—ibid., 92.

108   *Parsons' viewing of* Kane: Parsons, *Tell It,* 139; *Time,* January 27, 1941; Lebo, 139–40; Nasaw, 567–68.

109   "Hearst Objects to Welles Film"—*New York Times,* January 11, 1941.

111   "Mr. Hearst says if"—Brady, 280; Higham, *Orson Welles,* 169; Lebo, 138; Callow, 531. As late as 1991 Hearst's son William Jr. was still blithely attributing the fuss over *Kane,* including the threats against the studio bosses, exclusively to Parsons personally (see Hearst and Casserly, 185–87). His father, he contends,

was no more than a bemused bystander in the affair: "My father told me that he never made any effort to stop the film. . . . Speculation that he ordered Louella or Walter Winchell to 'get' people was nonsense." It was Parsons on her own "who raised all kinds of hell. . . . She masterminded attacks on almost everyone connected with it." From the little he does say, William Jr. must have been ignorant of the most basic facts of the affair, as laid out in this and earlier books.

112   "Nobody has taken the trouble"—*PM* (New York), February 16, 1941. Commenting on the spectacle of "Hollywood's great men taking to a bomb shelter" in the face of Hearst's threats, Hecht adds approvingly, "Mr. Schaeffer has, however, not joined this rush for immunity. He is still battling for the release of the film he fathered."

114   *Kitty Foyle and the* Mirror: Ads for *Kitty Foyle* ran right through January, nor was the serialized novel interrupted. A favorable review of the movie appeared on January 9.

114   "A Tempest in Hollywood's Teapot"—*New York Herald-Tribune,* January 19, 1941. At this time, January 1941, World War II in Europe had been underway more than a year. Pearl Harbor and America's entry into it was still almost another year away.

116   "Foreign Actors Crowding Americans"—*San Francisco Chronicle,* January 9, 1941. The threat to make an issue of the "alien invasion" of Hollywood built on an existing situation, to then low-key. A story in *PM* (August 20, 1940) reported that U.S. Secretary of Labor Frances Perkins had "made a quiet investigation . . . there was no public statement but Madame Perkins, it was said, was not pleased." See also Nasaw, 568.

116   "I wonder, in Hollywood's quest . . . In 1940 we've had"—*San Francisco Chronicle,* January 9, 1941.

118   "the town is threatened . . . If the trouble becomes"—
       New York Times, January 19, 1941.

119   *Senator Wheeler: San Francisco Chronicle,* January 25,
       1941.

119   "There was only one copy"—*Friday* magazine, Janu-
       ary 17, 1941, as quoted in Lebo, 135. Welles later wrote
       a brief reply to this article, of course denying any link
       between movie and Hearst. It was published in *Friday,*
       February 14, 1941 (reprinted in Gottesman, *Focus,* 67–
       68). Both article and reply are discussed at length in
       Lebo, 134–36.

121   *The theater chain boycott:* Carringer, *Making,* 117;
       Nasaw, 569; *PM,* May 1, 1941. There is disagreement
       over just how many individual theaters nationwide
       may have been involved. It may have been close to fif-
       teen hundred.

121   Kane *opening canceled:* Brady, 285–86.

122   *The Welles statement on* Kane: Brady, 283–85, prints
       the document in full. Curiously for so able a biogra-
       pher, Brady himself seems to have been partially per-
       suaded by Welles' subtle sophistry. He comments that
       even *if* the statement was an "entirely subjective and
       self-serving attempt" to obscure the truth, it was still
       "a fascinating interpretation of the film's ideation"
       (285). Not in the least. Welles' hugger-mugger reason-
       ing in this statement was first and last an effort to blot
       out *Kane*'s blatant Hearst background, everything he
       said obviously coming *after* the fact. Welles' most bra-
       zen assertion, surely, was that he *invented* Kane's col-
       lection mania as a way of accounting for the preserva-
       tion of the Rosebud sled.

Chapter 7. Waters Rising

128   *The Hearst meeting of February 1941:* Both the fact and
       the timing of this meeting, and its location, are my

own conclusions from the existing documents. Given *what* happened shortly after this date (see below), such a gathering, or say war-council, was necessary.

130   "has been watched with a good deal"—*Photoplay,* August 1941. For Welles and the draft see Higham, *Orson Welles,* 162–63, 176; Callow 560–61. The New York newspaper *PM* reported (April 14, 1941) that "a woman who said she was Louella Parsons" telephoned Welles' draft board "and demanded to know why" the star had not been inducted. No source or date for the call is given, and it is unlikely that Parsons, if it was her, would have identified herself. But that Hearst through his intermediaries did put pressure on Welles' draft board to call him up can be taken as certain.

131   *The attack on Schaeffer:* Fowler as quoted in Gottesman, *Focus,* 88. See also Nasaw, 570.

132   *Private showings of* Kane: Brady 299–300, 303; Carringer, *Making,* 115. Apparently there were several such private showings, on both coasts, involving viewers in the hundreds if not thousands. Comments Brady: "Schaeffer needed an accurate estimate of the film's worth [to use] as ammunition with RKO's board of directors" (299).

132   "It is with exceeding regret"—*Newsweek,* March 14, 1941.

134   "As in some grotesque . . . would break all the rules"—*Time,* March 17, 1941.

135   "To a film industry"—*Life,* March 17, 1941.

135   "might not think so—*Hollywood Reporter* in *The Motion Picture Herald,* March 17, 1941.

136   *The attack on Welles:* Brady, 289–93; Callow, 555–58; Higham, *Orson Welles,* 175; Thomson, 191–92. Nasaw (571) thinks to defend Hearst in this ugly incident by charging that Richard Wright, author of the novel *Native Son* on which the Welles-directed play was

based, was a member of the Communist Party. He also styles the government-sponsored Free Company as "a leftist group of radio writers and directors," and adds that some of its members "were affiliated with groups approved by *The Daily Worker.*" He gives no further information about the group or its aims, nor does he name any of the actors or writers involved. (For a look at how Hearst biography in general has handled the *Citizen Kane* matter see Appendix B).

137   "Legion Blasts Radio Drama Series"—*Milwaukee Sentinel,* April 13, 1941. Two other plays in the series in particular, said the paper, had been condemned by the Legion, "The Mole on Lincoln's Cheek" and "An American Crusader." No further comment is offered as to content, authors, or the grounds for objections. For how the story and the attack played on the west coast see Hearst's *San Francisco Examiner,* April 12–15, 1941, which also invokes the American Legion.

138   "The fighting spirit of the American Legion"— *Milwaukee Sentinel,* April 16, 1941. The headline on this story is "Welles Radio Play Series Legion Target." A subhead reads, "Communistic Tinge Seen by Veterans' Posts in East." One Legion official in Brooklyn stated that, "The name itself, Free Company, sounds suspiciously communistic. We would like to see the press bring out facts as to who pays for this time. . . . We would suggest that the Federal Communications Commission inquire immediately into these broadcasts." Carringer (*Making,* 115) states concerning the Hearst angle that "not coincidentally, a Hearst reporter was publicity chief for the Legion," but cites no source.

139   "severely criticizes Orson Welles"—*Milwaukee Sentinel,* April 18, 1941. The headline reads, "Called to Act on Plays by Welles." The final *Sentinel* story in the

matter appeared on April 20, headed "Legion Stand on Welles Indorsed." The endorser was a Chicago Legion commander who insisted that steps be taken "to stop this type of unnecessary program."

139   "William Randolph Hearst is conducting"—The statement is quoted whole in Brady, 291–92.

139   "then, too, is George M. Cohan"—*Pittsburgh Press,* April 24, 1941.

140   "the campaign against Mr. Welles"—*New York Times,* as quoted in Brady, 291.

140   "If it weren't sad"—*Chicago Sun Times,* April 27, 1941.

140   "Hearst and the people"—*New York Herald-Tribune,* September 11, 1951, as quoted in Higham, *Films of Orson Welles,* 21.

141   "They were really after me"—Rosenbaum, 85–86. Of course any attempt to research Welles' claim now would be a waste of time and effort, even as to whether it occurred in Pittsburgh or elsewhere. Who the detective was who heard about the plot, if there was one, whether the police did anything to interfere, which Hearst paper was involved, are interesting but unsolvable questions. Welles concludes his comment in the 1982 interview by saying that the instigator of the plot wasn't Hearst himself. It was "a hatchet man from the local Hearst paper who thought he would advance himself by doing it" (86). That's what he thought in 1982, when he'd mellowed and tended somewhat to pardon Hearst. It wasn't what he thought in 1941. Also it needs to be stated again that no local Hearst editor anywhere in the country would dare pull off such a criminal stunt without direct orders from San Simeon.

At least one contemporary report mentions Hearst operatives as shadowing Welles. While in Palm Springs for a brief rest in the spring of 1941, "he has been dogged in G-man style by Hearst photographers. Friday he and Delores Del Rio, whom it is said he may soon marry, stopped on the street to talk to a little boy. Just then a *Herald* photographer who had been trailing Welles for several days swooped by and snapped the scene from his moving car. When Welles saw the car speed by he shrugged his shoulders. 'Silly,' he said, 'I would gladly have posed for him'" (*PM*, April 14, 1941).

142 *Welles and* Native Son: Callow, 540–54; Brady, 294–98; Higham, *Orson Welles,* 165–66, 181–82; Houseman, *Front and Center,* 461–67, 470–74.

142 "It is as if the theater"—*New York Times,* March 25, 1941. The reviewer was Brooks Atkinson.

142 "The theater, that slumbering giant"—quoted in Callow, 552.

142 "Orson Welles is the greatest"—*New York World-Telegram,* March 25, 1941. The reviewer was Sidney Whipple. "Stark Drama Stamped with Genius," declared the review's headline of Welles. More than one critic, however, complained that director Welles had gone too far in sacrificing depth and significance in order to increase the dramatic impact. See Callow, 551, for some discussion.

143 "The kid has done it again"—*San Francisco Chronicle,* March 29, 1941. Hobart also notes that two prominent New York critics, Burns Mantle and Brooks Atkinson, contributed raves, but two others, Richard Watts and John Mason Brown, of equal stature with the first two, had with obvious reluctance expressed "some grave reservations." The current romantic interest of the just-divorced Welles, Dolores Del Rio, was also on hand, "making a glamorous entrance down the aisle."

144 *The RKO board meeting:* Based on information found in several sources: Carringer, *Making,* 112–15; Callow,

557–59; Leaming, 209–11; Rosenbaum, 85–87; Brady, 300–303; Nasaw, 569–71. For the editing out of the three minutes, see Brady, 302; Lebo, 143; and Carringer, *Making,* 112–13. What they concerned is not explained; see Carringer for some discussion of probabilities.

146 *The offer of Louis Mayer to buy* Kane: Brady, 288; Lebo, 141; Higham, *Orson Welles,* 171; Higham, *Merchant of Dreams,* 309; Kael, 5–6; Nasaw, 569. None of these state openly that Mayer was acting directly for Hearst, or that the money came from him. As Brady puts it, "Whether with Hearst's money backing him or a pool of cash pledged by a group of Hollywood producers, as it has often been surmised, or his own money, is not known." But some things may be taken as too obvious for argument. The idea of buying and destroying *Kane,* and the nearly one million dollars needed to do it, certainly came from Hearst. Mayer and his fellow moguls merely served as go-betweens.

147 *Welles' threat to sue RKO:* Brady, 300–301, and Lebo, 151–52, offer detailed coverage of this incident, but like most others they fail to understand that it was just another publicity gimmick cooked up between Welles and Schaeffer intended also to pressure the RKO board. On March 11, Welles in New York City called a press conference at his hotel, the Ambassador, and a large crowd of newsmen and photographers responded (*New York Times,* March 12). Leaving the grounds vague, he demanded that RKO immediately set a firm release date for *Kane.* At the same time he threatened to bring suit against Hearst himself for claming to be the original of Kane ("It is my duty as an artist and a citizen to sue")—proof enough that the whole affair was a set-up.

148 "For me to stand by"—*Motion Picture Herald,* March 14, 1941.

Chapter 8. Flood Tide

151 Kane *premier at the Palace:* My picture of the theater that night and the festivities is based on contemporary photographs, also Fowler, 100, and Callow, 561. Curiously, while many papers had critics on hand to review the picture, so far as I can find none gave a *social* description of the glamorous doings that night. Equally strange, not one of the many books and articles on Welles and *Kane* offers more than a brief mention of the premier, surely one of the most significant and potentially interesting in Hollywood history.

152 *The* Kane *souvenir booklet:* Reproduced whole in Lebo, 218–36. On two of the twenty-eight pages, ten members of the *Kane* cast are briefly profiled. The cover is a large headshot of Welles. Additional copies, states a note at the end, were available for 25 cents apiece.

153 *Welles ducking out:* Rosenbaum, 48, quotes Welles himself in a private conversation: "I went to the premier and went right out the side door when it started, the way I always do."

155 *First reviews of* Kane *read by Welles:* These are all dated May 2, 1941, and are sufficiently identified in my text. The papers quoted, I think, would have been the only ones available to him that morning.

164 "of fabulous screen stature"—*Journal of Commerce,* May 8, 1941.

164 "sacrifice of simplicity"—*Chicago Tribune,* May 8, 1941. The reviewer, Mae Tince, did find something to like: "The film has considerable suspense of a whodunit nature, tied up with a certain 'Rosebud.'" She also makes a sly reference to the Hearst imbroglio: "The usual foreword disclaiming intentional identification of the picture's characters with persons living or dead is conspicuous by its absence."

164   "Childe Orson"—*New Yorker,* May 3, 1941. I am assuming that Welles would have read this review while in Chicago, where he went on May 4 for *Kane's* Midwest premier.

166   *The Hollywood opening: Hollywood Reporter,* May 9, 1941; *Hollywood Citizen-News,* May 9, 1941; *Los Angeles Times,* May 9, 1941; Brady, 309.

166   "Motion picture celebs"—*Variety,* May 7, 1941.

167   "Mr. Welles' cinema bomb"—*Los Angeles Times,* May 9, 1941.

167   "jigsaw puzzle portrait of a man"—*Los Angeles Daily News,* May 10, 1941.

167   "so remarkable a photoplay"—*Hollywood Citizen-News,* May 9, 1941.

170   "an audience waiting breathless and alert . . . Because the real significance of *Kane*"—*New York Times,* May 4, 1941. Logically and sensibly, Crowther adds: "This corner is inclined to suspect that the enthusiasm with which Mr. Welles made the film—the natural bent of a first-class showman toward elegant and dramatic effects—rather worked against the logic of this story. The accomplishment of his purpose has been so completely impressive that it tends to blind the audience to the holes in the fabric." He also takes care to echo a point he made in the first review: "Everything about [the film] from a technical point of view is surprisingly magnificent."

A clearer, briefer expression of Crowther's thought is found in *Theatre Arts* where Rosamond Gilder contends that *Kane* offers "the picture of a man who is not really worth depicting, and here is the film's weakness. *Citizen Kane* depends for its importance on implications which are external to the movie itself. . . . His sway over the multitude is hinted at but never demonstrated, and yet it is only this power that lends the man stature enough" (June 2, 1941). In that little

267

phrase, "hinted at," perhaps resides the crux of the disagreement. Many subtle if fleeting moments in the picture signal Kane's power and his misuse of it (his building of Xanadu, for instance, his remark to an editor in 1898 that "I'll furnish the war," his remark that "if the headline is big enough it makes the story big enough," the choice between contradictory headlines when he loses an election, his hobnobbing with such as Hitler, his being interviewed on returning from a European trip when he smugly predicts there'll be no war, etc.). Whether these and similar sketched-in moments are sufficient to establish Kane's stature and its warped nature is what makes the argument. There are those who contend that the very sketchiness of these elements—quick brushstrokes of contrasting color—is what produces the effect of a powerful, unscrupulous personality who still is able to arouse sympathy and even to charm.

A review that appeared a few days after Crowther's second try (Joy Davidman in *The New Masses*, May 13, 1941), also supports him, but from a slightly different angle. Too much about Kane's professional life is left unstated, and "as a result the audience is left with a vast confusion as to what Kane really stands for in public life. This grotesque inadequacy in the midst of plenty keeps *Citizen Kane* from fulfilling its promise. In place of an analysis of Kane's true significance, the picture resorts to the trick of giving him a mysterious dying speech, supposed to be 'the real clue to Kane,' the sentimental explanation of which is coyly delayed until the fadeout." Not all reviewers, it seems, liked that Rosebud ending, finding it not at all dramatic but superficial and facile. Perhaps it is, in some moods. But as the climax to a supremely sinuous, two-hour movie—as opposed, say, to a psychology textbook—in its sudden, oblique suggestiveness it is perfect.

The handling of that final moment, in which the name Rosebud is revealed on the burning sled, was actually a last-minute decision. The shooting script (dated July 16 and 19, 1940, now preserved in the Theater Collection at the Wisconsin Historical Society, Madison) calls for the name to be highlighted as the workman picks it up from the pile of boxes, *before* he throws it into the flames. Who suggested the change is not now traceable.

171 "cold . . . unemotional, a puzzle"—*New York Sun,* May 2, 1941.

171 "a full and rich expression"—*New York World-Telegram,* May 2, 1941.

171 "elliptical method"—*New Yorker,* May 3, 1941.

171 *The San Francisco opening:* The unexplained postponement from May 14 to the twenty-seventh has not before been noticed. The *San Francisco Chronicle,* beginning on May 2, announced *Kane*'s San Francisco opening as set for the fourteenth ("It is almost upon us, chums! The amazing biography of 'Citizen Kane' that great and small character, will race across the screen of the Golden Gate Theater come Wednesday, May 14."). Large ads in the *Chronicle* on the next three days repeated the May 14 date. Then on the sixth appeared a brief announcement saying, as the headline expressed it, "*Citizen Kane* Is Mysteriously Postponed!" (see the next note). In the *Chronicle* on the eighteenth appeared the first announcement of the new date, the twenty-seventh, and at a different theater, the Geary. No explanation is given for the interruption.

172 "The picture WILL be shown"—*San Francisco Chronicle,* May 6, 1941.

172 "To begin, he entered the room"—*San Francisco Chronicle,* May 27, 1941.

174 "Welles and Hearst both arrived"—*Variety,* June 4, 1941. The story of the Hearst-Welles meeting in the

elevator has often been told, all versions emanating from Welles himself. See Lebo, 169, and Thomson, 195. In July 1984 it showed up in *Atlantic Monthly,* given a full page, half of it a drawing of the two men in an elevator.

176 "Take a bow!" — *Variety,* June 4, 1941.

176 "I was afraid you might" — *San Francisco Chronicle,* May 28, 1941.

176 "a skyrocket that explodes . . . You cannot watch this movie" — ibid. In that impressive run of early reviews a very long one in *Esquire* for August 1941, written by Gilbert Seldes, earned a prominent place. Seldes starts by saying that he has seen both the Welles play then running on Broadway, *Native Son,* and also *Citizen Kane* at the Palace. For him the two productions "were miles above anything in the theater or the movies of the year." In the picture he found a few soft spots, but he ends his long and particularly incisive review by offering this panegyric (in the process, however, overstating more than a little his knock on Hollywood): "The Hollywood product has become remarkably slick and smooth and polished . . . but there isn't any character to them, no stamina, no formative, energetic, pushing intelligence. . . . Orson Welles has shown Hollywood how to get those qualities. . . . He has made the movies young again by filling them with life."

In the influential *Theatre Arts* for June 1941 an equally telling notice added to the growing opinion, first voiced by Crowther in the *Times,* that the one true flaw in an otherwise great film was the character of Kane himself. The picture was "an exciting work, vital and imaginative, full of the unbridled energy which Orson Welles brings to every new medium he invades. . . . It is free of the bonds of precedent." However,

it is also, when all has been told, the picture of
a man who is not worth depicting, and here is
the film's weakness. *Citizen Kane* depends for
its importance on implications which are external to the movie itself. It acquires a sort of
reflected significance from the fact that it
might [!] be about a living man whom we all
know, a man who not only loves power but has
it, who wields a sinister influence on millions
of people through the medium of his newspapers and his money.

In the picture his sway over the multitude
is hinted at but never demonstrated; and yet it
is only this power which lends the man stature
enough to make him a vital subject. Without
his power he is an unpleasant rich man, nothing more. . . . Kane cannot be judged except on
his own film record, and by that standard he
must be found wanting.

Such an opinion, of course, was quite legitimate
criticism at the time and is still so today. Yet, again,
there are very many who take the opposite view, seeing Kane as a powerful whole, and for the very reason
that he is not festooned with detail, but evoked by
subtle indirection. Of course both groups are right.
The first thinks in terms of pure entertainment (does
it *work*?), the second in terms of pure art (it is whole
and consistent?).

178   "The bitter and doubting reaction—*Photoplay*, July
1941, 25–28. The writer was the magazine's editor, Ernest Heyn. In a brief, separate review of *Kane* in the
same issue he says that "The question of whether
twenty-six-year-old Orson Welles is a genius or an accident seems to be settled for all time. . . . The verdict

is Genius with great capital letters, with Hollywood paying homage to the skill and artistry abounding in *Citizen Kane*."

179 "the hottest thing in town"—*Variety,* May 7, 1941, 6, 9.

179 "not a smash"—*Variety,* May 14, 1941, 4, 11.

179 "one exception is *Citizen Kane . . .* receipts were very disappointing"—ibid., 18.

179 *Palace down to half its capacity: Variety,* June 11, 1941, 23. Nor was its competition overwhelming, such fare as *Love Crazy, Topper Returns, Blood and Sand, Penny Serenade, Devil Dogs of the Air,* and *Fantasia.*

181 "war jitters . . . the recent skid"—*Variety,* May 21, 1941, 7.

181 "Managers of theaters"—*Variety,* May 29, 1941, 15.

181 *Size of* Kane's *loss:* Brady, 311, Lebo, 180. As things went then in Hollywood, $150,000 was not a huge loss, except that RKO in 1941 was not in good shape financially.

Chapter 9. Last Chance

182 *Awards of 1941 to* Kane: *New York Times,* December 10, 1941; Brady, 310; Carringer, *Making,* 117. Adding to the favorable impact of those two awards was a poll taken by the *Hollywood Reporter* (May 12, 1941) offering voters a dozen categories beginning with Best Picture. *Kane* easily took that honor, as well as first place finishes in nine other categories, with Welles capturing Best Actor and Best Director. From all these early indications the public had good reason to expect, as it did, a similar sweep by *Kane* at the 1942 Academy Awards. The fact that it earned only a single top spot (Best Script) needs a more searching explanation than has so far been given it. My contention that the difference was made by Hearst's secret interference in the Academy voting may some day be demonstrated, perhaps

when the horde of unsorted, partially restricted Hearst papers at Bancroft Library, University of California, Berkeley, are finally arranged and studied.

183   *Academy Awards 1942: Variety,* February 26–27, 1942; *New York Times,* February 26–27, 1942; *San Francisco Chronicle,* February 27, 1942; Fontaine, 81, 144–47; Lebo, 178–80; Thomson, 211–13.

183   "while their sister guests"—*Variety,* March 4, 1942. Other news accounts make it seem that not just a few but most of the female stars present had dressed for the occasion: "Feminine stars yielded little to the informality, however. They appeared in evening dresses, adorned in furs, jewels, and flowers." The paper adds that, even so, the night "lacked most of its glamour and fanfare" (*Milwaukee Journal,* February 27, 1942).

184   "We must re-win every foot"—*Milwaukee Journal,* February 27, 1942. *Variety* adds that Wilkie, "paid tribute to the Americanism of the leaders of the film industry and commended their showmanship in producing films that the people want" (March 4, 1942).

185   "The Biggest Upset"—*Variety,* March 4, 1942.

186   "That most of the 6,000 extras . . . The brush given the boy wonder"—ibid. The one Welles biographer who mentions the extras vote and its negative effect on Welles is Callow, 577. His only comment: "(Why? He had hired 796 of them on *Kane*)." The number may or may not be accurate. It seems high.

187   "There was fierce atmosphere"—Thomson, 213. No source is cited for the description, though expressed in rather definite terms. Perhaps it is a combination of Carringer, *Making,* 117; Brady, 311; and a bit of surmise.

187   "At first mention of the title"—Brady, 311. So far as can be told, this (1989) is the first appearance in print of the claim that the 1942 Academy Awards audience

was openly hostile to Welles, at least some part of it. The idea has since been picked up and used by others, still lacking a source, or even a reasonable basis.

188 *Possible role of Hearst in the extras vote:* To those familiar with Hearst's cutthroat methods—in 1942 still unsoftened by age—the idea that he and his money engineered Welles' defeat at the Academy Awards will come as no shock, in fact will seem only a matter of simple logic. As stated, 1942 was the first year that movie extras were given a voice in the voting. Just how that curious move originated, and why, no one seems able to discover. See also Lebo, 179–80.

189 *The auto accident:* Meryman, 282–84, Kael, 79–80. For whatever reason, it is not reported or referred to in any of the Welles or Hearst biographies. The secretary in the Gershwin car was Peggy Morton, the laundress Annie Jones.

190 "Mrs. Gershwin Hurt"—*Los Angeles Examiner,* March 12, 1943.

191 "Hold Writer in Hollywood Car Collision"—*New York Mirror,* March 14, 1943. A photograph of Mankiewicz accompanies the story. The other two women in the car, it states without authority, were "also reported injured." According to Kael (80), Mankiewicz had known the Gershwins "for years," both in Hollywood and New York, and it is true that in 1932 he worked on the screen adaptation of George Gershwin's *Girl Crazy* (Meryman, 331). Kael also states, on the authority of playwright Marc Connolly, that Mankiewicz after his release on bail that day and his return home, was sent by his wife over to the Gershwin house with an offering of flowers: "The house was full of reporters, and Ira Gershwin was serving them drinks and trying to keep things affable. Mankiewicz went upstairs to see Lee, who was lying in bed with her head

bandaged" (80). Whatever Mankiewicz might have said to Mrs. Gershwin that night by way of apology didn't work, for she and her husband brought suit against him asking $50,000 damages. She lost on the resulting hung jury (Meryman, 284).

Also recorded by Kael is the fact that Hearst actually succeeded in doing hurt to Mankiewicz as he fully intended. "Although he got through the mess of the trial all right, the hounding by the Hearst papers took its toll, and his reputation was permanently damaged" (80). The fact that this ugly episode is not covered by either of Hearst's principal biographers, Swanberg and Nasaw, and appears nowhere else in Hearst literature, I think deserves particular emphasis. Several reasons for the omission can be guessed, of course, though none really serves. Two years after *Kane* closed, a failure, Hearst is seen still trying to destroy one of the movie's two writers, in good part succeeding, yet no Hearst commentator reports it? Meryman, unfortunately, makes something of a joke of the whole thing, quoting Mankiewicz's tired defensive quips.

191   "Screen Writer Faces Drunk"—*Milwaukee Sentinel,* March 14, 1943, page one. The Mankiewicz quotes in the story, and those attributed to the arresting officer, are printed by the *Sentinel* in *boldface* type. This of course was not the usual style of the *Sentinel,* nor of any other paper. Hearst's vindictive small-mindedness and blind fury are rather starkly revealed by the fact. The paper's reference to the 1931 Beverly Hills traffic ticket given Mankiewicz has something wrong with it. The Mankiewiczes were not then living in Beverly Hills.

193   "Drunk Driving Hearing"—*Milwaukee Sentinel,* March 15, 1943, page one. The police chief is quoted describing the accident: "Only Mrs. Gershwin's quick and desperate attempt to swing her lighter vehicle out

275

of the path of the oncoming heavier convertible coupe, which was plunging at her, saved lives." He added, a bit vaguely, that the radiator ornament on the Mankiewicz car "came within an inch or two" of the other car's windshield.

194 "other members of the [Hearst] chain"—*Newsweek,* March 29, 1943.

194 *Mankiewicz's trial:* Meryman, 284. Mankiewicz's lawyer was Jerry Geisler, well-known attorney to the stars, a specialist in beating the rap.

195 *Mankiewicz's last screen credits:* Meryman, 335. The four pictures were *The Enchanted Cottage* with Dorothy McGuire and Robert Young (coauthor), *The Spanish Main* with Maureen O'Hara and Paul Henreid (coauthor), *A Woman's Secret* with Maureen O'Hara and Melvyn Douglas, and *The Pride of St. Louis* with Dan Dailey and Joanne Dru.

195 "Like all the cast"—Warrick, *Confessions,* 61. Her banishment from the Hearst press, she says, was finally lifted through the intercession of Louella Parsons.

195 *The* Kane *cast and Hearst:* None of *Kane's* other leading players left any record of interference in their careers by Hearst. Joseph Cotton later wrote an autobiography but had nothing to say on the topic, and his career shows only a steady record of accomplishment. The same may be said of Sloane, Collins, Coulouris, Moorehead, and the lesser players.

196 "Dorothy Commingore, green-eyed"—*Cue,* June 12, 1941. About the same time *Photoplay* gave her a two-page spread. Earlier, the popular *Colliers* magazine carried a lengthy profile of her by Kyle Crichton ("No unknown ever came so far so fast").

198 Unexpected Uncle *and* Valley of the Sun: Both pictures were released to good notices in 1942. Commingore's selection for both films was reported in *Variety,* May 14, 1941, and August 10, 1941.

199 "Unfortunately, Dorothy Commingore"—*New York Times*, July 3, 1944.

199 *The arrest for soliciting: New York Post*, March 20, 1953; *San Francisco Chronicle*, March 20, 1953; obituary, *Los Angeles Times*, January 2, 1972. The United Press story, carried by the *San Francisco Chronicle*, was for some unknown reason ignored by some other leading papers, for instance the *Chicago Tribune* and the *New York Times*.

199 "she began to drink heavily"—Warrick, *Confessions*, 60. Warrick also gives what she represents as Orson Welles' opinion, privately expressed during the filming of *Kane*, that Commingore's talent was limited. Supposedly he subjected her, on and off the set, to a "discourteous contempt that was often painful to watch." When Warrick objected, Welles explained that he was merely preparing Commingore for her role: "I treat her that way because she has got to hate my guts when we get to the later scenes." But an actress need not "be bleeding to show pain," commented Warrick, bringing from Welles this rejoinder: "That's just the point. She is *not* an actress. She *is* Susan Alexander, and she'll probably end up just like the woman she's playing. . . . I'm not mistreating her. I treat her exactly as she *expects* to be treated. She wouldn't respect anything else" (59). Warrick is here calling on a forty-year-old memory. If her report is accurate, how it fits into the possibility of Hearst's involvement is hard to say.

200 *Called by the House Committee:* Commingore refused "on constitutional grounds to answer key questions of the Committee," asserting a "passionate loyalty to my country" (*Los Angeles Times*, January 2, 1972).

200 "I've had nothing but trouble lately"—*San Francisco Chronicle*, March 20, 1953. This same quote from Commingore, in precisely the same words, also appears

in the *New York Post* story of the same date, though the two stories came from different sources. The *Post* story was a "special," the *Chronicle* taken from the UP wire. The remainder of the two versions bears no such similarity, except for the mention of "a dark place."

200   "Deputy Sheriffs William Baker"—*New York Post,* March 20, 1953. The story, datelined "Hollywood, March 19," carries no byline.

202   "Miss Commingore was arrested"—*San Francisco Chronicle,* March 20, 1953. The story adds that "She pleaded not guilty in Municipal Court, but was jailed when unable to pay the $500 bail set by the court. Trial was set for April 10." There was no trial because, as was reported in the *Los Angeles Times* obituary, "the case was dismissed on a motion by the district attorney and she was committed to the Los Angeles County General Hospital's psychopathic ward for treatment as an alcoholic" (January 2, 1972).

202   *Death of Commingore: New York Times,* December 31, 1971; *Los Angeles Times,* January 2, 1972; *The Day* (New London, Connecticut), December 30 and 31, 1971. The first story in *The Day* is a one-paragraph announcement of the death of "Mrs. Dorothy Crowe, 58, of Lord's Point." A story the next day identifies her as the actress Dorothy Commingore, but credits the *New York Times* for the information. Today she has again been forgotten in her home area: the Stonington Historical Society reports that it is not aware of *Kane's* star having been a neighbor, and has no information about her.

202   *Previous marriages:* Arriving in Hollywood in 1939 as a protégé of Charlie Chaplin, by 1940 Commingore had married screenwriter Richard Collins. Two children were born before their divorce in 1946. Her second husband was magazine editor Theodore Strauss. They

were married in 1948 and divorced two years later. When and where she married John Crowe (identified in the *Los Angeles Times* obituary as "a post office worker") is not presently known.

203 *Hearst's role in Commingore's failure:* Since Hearst died in August 1951 he could not have had a direct hand in her 1953 arrest. But he had ten years (1941 to 1951) to work her destruction in films, and it is clear that something or somebody *did* so. After her performance in *Kane,* judging by available sources, her future in Hollywood seemed assured. By itself, therefore, the fact that three years passed between *Kane* and her second movie, *The Hairy Ape,* needs *some* explanation besides the possibility that she may simply have failed to impress potential employers. Her fall seems much too swift and precipitous to have been without external cause.

204 "Drinking neat scotch"—Guiles, 8.

204 *Death of Hearst:* Guiles, 3–13; Davies, 250–52; Nasaw, 598–601; Swanberg, 617–18; Tebbel, 218–19; and newspaper obituaries cited below.

204 "I asked where he was"—Guiles, 13; Nasaw, 600; *Life,* August 19, 1951.

204 "his friend and confidante"—*New York Times, Baltimore Sun, San Francisco Chronicle, Chicago Tribune,* all for August 15, 1951.

204 "the property of the former actress"—*New York Herald-Tribune,* August 17, 1951. It is an Associated Press story, thus can be found in many papers, sometimes a bit rewritten.

205 *Praise for Hearst:* See the round-ups of favorable quotes in the *New York Times,* August 15, 1951, and the *San Francisco Chronicle,* August 15, 1951. Most obituaries in other papers carried several.

205 "alternately praised and damned—*New York Herald Tribune,* August 17, 1951.

205 "He brought shock and bitter outrage"—*New York Herald-Tribune,* August 15, 1951.

206 "the greatest figure in American journalism . . . ushered in the modern era"—*San Francisco Herald-Examiner,* August 15, 1951. Quoted here from the *New York Times,* August 15, 1951.

206 "it was merely a question"—*Nation,* August 25, 1951. The editorial is preceded by a full-page reprint of a piece the magazine had published as early as 1898 condemning the day's growing threat of "yellow journalism." Obviously aimed in particular at the Hearst papers, it refers in not-so-veiled terms to Hearst himself as "a black-guard boy with several millions of dollars at his disposal," who was then exerting more influence, in a way, "than all the statesmen and philosophers and professors in the country." The one shocking characteristic of such "yellow journals" is that they are "for the first time in American history an *irresponsible* force. . . . Every other influence in the community not openly criminal acknowledges some sort of restraint. . . . From every such discipline or restraint, except libel suits, the yellow journalist is absolutely free. His one object is to circulate widely and make money."

208 *Hearst's targeting of Welles:* The silent assumption in Welles' biography is that after the 1941 failure of *Kane,* and its withdrawal from public exhibition, Hearst let up on him. But that assumption certainly needs rethinking. If Hearst, during the crucial decade of the forties up to his death in 1951, really was behind at least some of Welles' difficulties as a filmmaker, the continuing effects of that baleful influence would likely have made themselves felt long afterwards. In that case another part of the puzzle of Welles' steady decline is put in place. While his personal shortcomings might have

been enough to derail him, he was also, in some degree, one more sad victim of the vengeful Hearst. As Hedda Hopper had warned him, he *didn't* get away with it.

Chapter 10. Then Is Heard No More

211 *Death of Welles:* Obituaries, all for October 11, 1985, in the *Los Angeles Times, San Francisco Chronicle, Chicago Tribune, Milwaukee Sentinel, Minneapolis Star-Tribune, Denver Post, New York Times, New York Herald-Tribune;* also Brady, 590–91, and Thomson, 354, 421.

212 "was one of largely unfulfilled promise"—*New York Times,* October 11, 1985, 1. The same story notes, however, that in 1975 Welles was given a Lifetime Achievement Award by the American Film Institute, and only the year before his death had been given the Griffith Award by the Directors Guild of America.

212 "his talents remained unfulfilled"—*Los Angeles Times,* October 10, 1985.

212 "He became virtually unemployable"—*Los Angeles Times,* October 11, 1985. The story adds that in Welles' later years "he was honored again and again by the film establishment . . . and at film festivals all around the world."

212 "cut short through a combination"—*Chicago Tribune,* October 11, 1985. Mentioned also is a 1970 award to Welles, a special Oscar for "superlative artistry and versatility in the creation of motion pictures."

212 "For his failure to realize his dreams"—*New York Times,* October 11, 1985.

214 "Why couldn't Welles hang on"—*Newsweek,* October 21, 1985.

214 "Orson Welles was, I think"—quoted in McClelland, 404.

215 "His Kind of Town, Kenosha Wasn't"—*Kenosha News,* October 11, 1985. Writer Jensen goes on to correct some of the more colorful tales Welles told about the eccentric ways of his family in Kenosha, particularly regarding his several aunts and his father. His last visit to town, says Jensen, came in July 1942 when he returned for his grandmother's funeral: "He arrived quietly by train from Chicago, took a cab from the station to Hanson's Funeral Home. Then in unseemly haste, some recall, he left for the last time." This visit, however, is not recorded in Welles' biography, and in fact that July he was still in Brazil working on his South American picture, being filmed in Rio. It is possible that he did reach home by month's end and went straight to Kenosha. The dead grandmother, though, he intensely disliked, so that some believe he wouldn't and didn't go to her funeral (Callow, 63–64; Higham, *Orson Welles,* 24–27).

In this same issue of the *Kenosha News* was reprinted the whole lengthy obituary account from the *Los Angeles Times,* along with a photograph of the house where he was born in Kenosha.

Longest and most detailed of all the Welles obituary-biographies was that in *Variety,* October 16, 1985. It called him "a Renaissance Man," and said that he "spent much of his life living down the fact that he had conquered the worlds of radio, theater, and film by the time he was twenty-five."

217 "a marvelous little corner in time"—Rosenbaum, 92. In this same passage Welles refers to Grand Detour as "one of those lost worlds, one of those Edens that you get thrown out of." (For a description of the town itself in some detail see Callow, 23–27.) The interviewer unfortunately failed to pursue the tantalizing opening unexpectedly handed him, so nothing more is heard

of the deserted dance hall. "You do have a fondness for things of the past," was the interviewer's sole comment, to which Welles deftly responded by leading the conversation away from Grand Detour. "Oh, yes," he guardedly replied, "for that Eden people lose . . . it's a theme that interests me. A nostalgia for the garden — it's a recurring theme in all our civilization." Apparently he'd grown suddenly uncomfortable with the personal revelation he'd let slip.

Appendix B. *Citizen Kane* in Hearst Biography

225 "ill-considered attempt" — Tebbel, 287–88.

226 "raised a cinematic storm . . . to having his own private life" — Swanberg, 497–98.

227 "The pressure against . . . Louis Mayer, never" — ibid., 497.

228 "It is possible that Welles" — Nasaw, 566.

228 "Out of loyalty to Hearst" — ibid., 568.

228 "a leftist group of writers and directors" — ibid., 571.

229 "in a gesture of conciliation . . . the only other guy in Hollywood" — ibid., 570.

229 "Hearst was able" — Swanberg, 502.

229 "never having seen one of Marion's films" — Nasaw, 573–74.

230 "Kane is a cartoon-like caricature" — ibid., 574.

230 "the real story of Hearst" — ibid.

231 "in the whole history of the screen" — Rosenbaum.

231 "I never saw the picture *Citizen Kane* . . . I heard about Aldous Huxley" — Davies, 264–65.

232 "an old man trembling" — Guiles, 313.

232 "pretended that *Kane* . . . None of her friends" — ibid., 317, 321.

Selected Bibliography

Listed here are those printed sources, books and articles, which contributed directly to my subject and which are cited by short titles in the notes. Simple newspaper reports cited in the notes are *not* repeated here. Also listed are a few titles whose value lay in providing stimulus and background.

Ager, C., "*Citizen Kane* Rates A Furore!" [review of *Kane*], *Chicago Tribune,* May 8, 1941.

Anger, K., *Hollywood Babylon,* Dutton, 1984.

Anon., "Marvelous Boy," *Time,* May 9, 1938.

_____, "Orson Delivers," *Friday,* January 17, 1941.

_____, "Citizen Welles Raises Kane," *Time,* January 27, 1941.

_____, "In His First Film Orson Welles Breaks All the Rules," *Life,* March 17, 1941.

_____, "Orson Welles Enters! No Fuss, No Fanfare but Room Vibrates!" *San Francisco Chronicle,* May 27, 1941.

_____, "The Truth about the Draft in Hollywood," *Photoplay,* August 1941.

Baker, R., *The Dark Historic Page: Social Satire in the Novels of Aldous Huxley,* University of Wisconsin Press, 1982.

Baldanza, F., "Huxley and Hearst," in *Essays on California Writers,* edited by C. Crow, Bowling Green University Press, 1978.

Barnes, H., "Citizen Kane," [review of *Kane*], *New York Herald-Tribune,* May 2, 1941.

Bates, R., and S. Bates, "Fiery Speech in a World of Shadows: Rosebud's Impact on Early Audiences," *Cinema Journal* (winter) 1987.

Bedford, S., *Aldous Huxley: A Biography,* Knopf, 1974.

Beja, M., ed., *Perspectives on Orson Welles,* Hall, 1995.

Black, S. T., *Child Star,* McGraw, 1989.

Bleyer, W., *Main Currents in the History of American Journalism,* Houghton Mifflin, 1927.

Brady, F., *Citizen Welles,* Scribner's, 1989.

Callow, S., *Orson Welles: The Road to Xanadu,* London, 1995.

Cantril, H., *The Invasion from Mars: A Study in the Psychology of Panic,* Princeton University Press, 1940.

Carey, G., *Anita Loos: A Biography,* Knopf, 1988.

Carlson, O., and E. Bates, *Hearst: Lord of San Simeon,* Viking, 1936.

Carringer, R., "The Scripts of *Citizen Kane,*" *Critical Inquiry,* 5, 1978, repr. in Gottesman, *Perspectives,* 141–71.

———, *The Making of Citizen Kane,* University of California Press, 1985.

Chaplin, C., *My Autobiography,* Simon & Schuster, 1964.

Churchill, D., "Bearded Bogeyman Goes to Hollywood," *New York Times,* August 20, 1939.

———, "Orson Welles Scares Hollywood," *New York Times,* January 17, 1941.

Clark, V., *Aldous Huxley and Film,* Scarecrow Press, 1987.

Cotton, J., *Vanity Will Get You Somewhere,* Mercury, 1987.

Coulouris, G., "The D—with Orson," *Punch,* May 18, 1960.

Cowie, P., *The Cinema of Orson Welles,* Barnes, 1965.

Crisler, B., "A Week of Orson Welles," *New York Times,* January 28, 1940.

Crowther, B., *Hollywood Rajah,* Doubleday, 1982.

————, "Orson Welles's Controversial 'Citizen Kane' Proves a Sensational Film at Palace," [review of *Kane*], *New York Times,* May 2, 1941.

————, "The Ambiguous *Citizen Kane,*" [second review of *Kane*], *New York Times,* May 4, 1941.

Davies, M., *The Times We Had: Life with W. R. Hearst,* Bobbs, 1975.

Dunaway, D., *Huxley in Hollywood,* Harper, 1989.

Eells, G., *Hedda and Louella,* Putnam's, 1972.

Escourt, C., Jr., "The Shooting about Mr. Orson Welles," *San Francisco Chronicle,* March 16, 1941.

Fadiman, C., "Invitation to Immortality," [review of *After Many a Summer*], *New Yorker,* January 27, 1940.

Ferguson, O., "Citizen Welles," *New Republic,* June 2, 1941.

Fitzgerald, F., "Pat Hobby and Orson Welles," *Esquire,* May 1940.

Flint, L., *The Conscience of a Newspaper,* D. Appleton and Company, 1925.

Fontaine, J., *No Bed of Roses,* Morrow, 1978.

Fowler, R., *Orson Welles: A First Biography,* Pendulum, 1946.

Friedrich, O., *City of Nets: A Portrait of Hollywood in the 1940s,* Harper's, 1986.

Geist, K., *Pictures Will Talk: The Life and Films of Joseph L. Mankiewicz,* Scribner's, 1978.

Gladden, W., *Tainted Newspapers,* New York, 1914.

Gottesman, R., *Focus on* Citizen Kane, Prentice-Hall, 1971.

————, *Perspectives on* Citizen Kane, Hall, 1996.

Griffin, M., *From Where I Sit,* Arbor House, 1982.

Guiles, F. L., *Marion Davies: A Biography,* McGraw-Hill, 1972.

Hearst, W. R., Jr., and J. Casserley, *The Hearsts, Father and Son,* Rinehart, 1991.

Heyn, E., "Man of the Moment," *Photoplay*, July 1941.

Higham, C., *The Films of Orson Welles*, University of California Press, 1970.

―――, *Orson Welles: The Rise and Fall of an American Genius*, St. Martin's Press, 1985.

―――, *Merchant of Dreams: Louis B. Mayer and MGM*, Fine, 1993.

Hobart, J., "A Critic in New York: John Hobart Goes to the Opening of a Welles Play," [review of *Native Son*], *San Francisco Chronicle*, March 28, 1941.

―――, "Mr. Welles' Cause Celebre," [review of *Kane*], *San Francisco Chronicle*, May 28, 1941.

Hopper, H., *From Under My Hat*, Doubleday, 1952.

―――, *The Whole Truth and Nothing But*, Doubleday, 1966.

Houseman, J., *Run-Through: A Memoir*, Simon & Schuster, 1972.

―――, *Front and Center*, Simon & Schuster, 1979.

Huxley, A., *After Many a Summer Dies the Swan*, Harper, 1939.

Isaacs, H., "Citizen Kane," [review of *Kane*], *Theatre Arts*, June 1941.

Jewell, R., *The RKO Story*, Arlington House, 1982.

Johnson, E., "Amor Dei in Hollywood," [review of *After Many a Summer*], *Kenyon Review*, December 1939.

Johnston, A., and F. Smith, "How to Raise a Child: The Education of Orson Welles, Who Didn't Need It," *Saturday Evening Post*, January 20, 27, February 3, 1940.

Kael, P., "Raising Kane," *New Yorker*, February 20, 27, 1971, repr. in *The Citizen Kane Book*, Little Brown, 1971.

Kauffman, S., and B. Henstell, *American Film Criticism: From the Beginning to* Citizen Kane, Liveright, 1972.

Leaming, B., *Orson Welles: A Biography*, Viking, 1985.

Lebo, H., *Citizen Kane: The 50th Anniversary Album*, Doubleday, 1990.

Lee, J., *History of American Journalism*, New York, 1917.

288

Lewis, O., *Fabulous San Simeon,* California Historical Society, 1960.

Loos, A., *A Girl Like I,* New York, 1969.

Lundberg, F., *Imperial Hearst: A Social Biography,* New York, 1936, Arno, 1970.

Maloney, R., "Orson Welles," *New Yorker,* October 9, 1938.

Maltin, L., *The Great American Radio Broadcast: Radio's Golden Age,* New American Library, 1997.

Marion, F., *Off with Their Heads: A Socioeconomic Tale of Hollywood,* Macmillan, 1972.

McBride, J., *Orson Welles,* Viking, 1972.

McClelland, D., *Forties Film Talk: An Oral History of Hollywood,* McFarland, 1992.

Meryman, R., *Mank: The Wit, World, and Life of Herman Mankiewicz,* Morrow, 1978.

Mosher, J., "Childe Orson," *New Yorker,* May 3, 1941.

Mulvey, L., *Citizen Kane,* London, 1992.

Murray, K., *The Golden Days of San Simeon,* Doubleday, 1971.

Naremore, J., *The Magic World of Orson Welles,* Oxford University Press, 1978.

Nasaw, D., *The Chief: The Life of W. R. Hearst,* Houghton, 2000.

Noble, P., *The Fabulous Orson Welles,* London, 1956.

Older, F., *William Randolph Hearst: American,* New York, 1936.

Othman, F., "*Citizen Kane* Previewed: Even Hollywood Now Admits the Man from Mars Is a Genius," [review of *Kane*], *San Francisco Chronicle,* April 11, 1941.

Parsons, L., *The Gay Illiterate,* Doubleday, 1945.

—————, *Tell It to Louella,* Putnam, 1961.

Payne, G., *History of Journalism in the U.S.,* D. Appleton and Company, 1920.

Powell, D., "The Life and Opinions of Orson Welles," *Sunday Times* (London), February 3, 1963.

Procter, B., *W. R. Hearst: The Early Years,* Oxford University Press, 1998.

Rosenbaum, J., ed., *This Is Orson Welles: Conversations with Peter Bogdanovich,* HarperCollins, 1992.

Sarlot, R., and F. Basten, *Life at the Marmont,* Roundtable, 1987.

Sklar, R., "Welles before *Kane:* Discourse on a Boy Genius," *Persistence of Vision,* no. 7, 1989.

Sorel, N., "Hearst and Welles," *Atlantic Monthly,* July 1984.

Staiger, J., ed., *The Studio System,* Rutgers University Press, 1995.

Swanberg, W. A., *Citizen Hearst,* Scribner's, 1961.

Taylor, J., *Orson Welles: A Celebration,* Little Brown, 1986.

Tebbel, J., *The Life and Good Times of W. R. Hearst,* Dutton, 1952.

Thomson, D., *Rosebud: The Story of Orson Welles,* Little Brown, 1996.

Tince, M., "*Citizen Kane* Fails to Impress Critic as Greatest Ever Filmed," *Chicago Tribune,* May 8, 1941.

Toland, G., "How I Broke the Rules in *Citizen Kane,*" *Popular Photography,* June 1941, repr. in Gottesman, *Focus,* 73–77.

———, "The Motion Picture Cameraman," *Theatre Arts,* September 1941.

Torrence, B., *Hollywood: The First Hundred Years,* New York Zoetrope, 1982.

Warner, J., *My First 100 Years In Hollywood,* Random House, 1965.

Warrick, R., *The Confessions of Phoebe Tyler,* Prentice-Hall, 1980.

———, "Memories of *Citizen Kane*", in McClelland, *Forties Film Talk.*

Welles, O., "*Citizen Kane* Is Not about Louella Parsons' Boss," *Friday,* February 14, 1941.

———, "Orson Welles on His Purpose in Making *Citizen Kane,*" in Gotteman, *Perspectives,* 23–26.

Wilkerson, M., *Public Opinion and the Spanish-American War,* Louisiana State University Press, 1932.

Winkler, J., *W. R. Hearst: An American Phenomenon,* Simon & Schuster, 1928.

————, *Hearst: A New Appraisal,* Hastings House, 1955.

Wood, B., *Orson Welles: A Bio-Bibliography,* Greenwood Press, 1990.

Index

293

294

A RAY AND PAT BROWNE BOOK

Series Editors
Ray B. Browne and Pat Browne